"There is always a book on the shelf…!"

Country Reminiscing: The Social Evolution of a Parish Community delightfully told through the History of its School; Lower Heath CE School

Roger West

Compiled and edited by Anne West

Grosvenor House
Publishing Limited

All rights reserved
Copyright © Roger West, 2025

The right of Roger West to be identified as the author of this
work has been asserted in accordance with Section 78
of the Copyright, Designs and Patents Act 1988

The book cover is copyright to Roger West

This book is published by
Grosvenor House Publishing Ltd
Link House
140 The Broadway, Tolworth, Surrey, KT6 7HT.
www.grosvenorhousepublishing.co.uk

This book is sold subject to the conditions that it shall not, by way of
trade or otherwise, be lent, resold, hired out or otherwise circulated
without the author's or publisher's prior consent in any form of
binding or cover other than that in which it is published and
without a similar condition including this condition being
imposed on the subsequent purchaser.

A CIP record for this book
is available from the British Library

Paperback ISBN 978-1-83615-263-7
Hardback ISBN 978-1-83615-264-4

Dedicated to the attendees of Lower Heath School and
Fauls Green Parishioners, Past, Present and Future

Author Roger West

Roger West Bio

Roger is a born and bred native of Lower Heath, North Shropshire. He was born in 1932 in a house, on what was once part of the Hills of Hawkestone Estate, built near the timber yard. At the age of 5 (1937) he attended Lower Heath School, leaving at the age of 14 in 1946. Unable to pursue college due to severe travel sickness, he "went to the tools" as an apprentice to the "Joiner, Wheelwright and Undertaker," Mr. George Ward who was based in Fauls Green.

After joining the Duke of Cornwall's Light Infantry Regiment to serve his National Service he was initially trained and stationed on Salisbury Plain. Roger then left for Germany to join the British Army of the Rhine (BAOR); patrolling the Rhine and monitoring the Minden Gap with his fellow soldiers. He travelled to different parts of Germany as a reserve for the Army football team and was lucky enough, to almost always, gain a place on the pitch. His love of football continues to this day, matched by his love and enthusiasm for local history especially the Hills of Hawkestone.

When George Ward retired, Roger started his own business as the local builder. This was more than a job for Roger, it was a way of life, enabling him to interview parishioners, collecting more stories from the past. Coupled with his passion for collecting old postcards and photographs of the area, it enabled him to write a detailed and entertaining history of Lower Heath School and the community it served and built.

Acknowledgements

I would like to express my thanks to all those who have provided or given access to the information required to write the Church Venture Articles and for Doreen Hopwood who persuaded me to write articles for the magazine all those years ago. Thanks also to those who have supported Anne in compiling this book, particularly Paul Ridgley. Many thanks to the Lower Heath school children and Fauls Green parishioners, far and near, past, and present, who willingly spent time reminiscing about their school times and their experiences growing up in this idyllic part of North Shropshire.

Special Thanks

To my wife Mary who has accompanied me through life since we met at the age of 14. Mary has been a constant nurturing support throughout our life's rich tapestry of events. Her patience knows no bounds.

Thanks to my daughters; Anne for compiling and editing the book and Kath for scanning photographs from my collection.

Roger West

Other Sources of Information

Collins Dictionary

Charities Commissioners Report dated 1824

Church Records

Harry Brown WWI Experiences

His Majesty's Inspectorate of Schools Reports

John Allen, Vicar of Prees and Archdeacon of Salop: A Memoir. R.M. Grier

Lower Heath School Log Book and Reports

Miss Thomas' Memoirs

Mrs. Bloor (former Headteacher) Notes

Mrs. Morrison (nee Sandford) Scrapbook

Oxford Dictionary

Rev. Brian Hill Pamphlet 1801 and 1804

Rogers Conversations with Parishioners

Shropshire Archives

The correspondence of Lady Elizabeth Hill

Wildings Postcards

https://www.cwgc.org/

https://www.iwm.org.uk/

https://www.nationalarchives.gov.uk/currency-converter/

Foreword

Strangers driving up through Fauls Green, are unlikely to be impressed by this sleepy little rural hamlet. They may notice a large building on their right, but often than not, miss the name "FAULS CHURCH HALL" over the door, as their eyes are drawn to the first signs of life on their left. They might notice our dear little church, on their right and a few more houses up bank, but, as the saying goes: "If they have blinked, they have missed it." The quietness belies the vibrant activity that goes on here when the scattered community comes together.

The parish is extensive, mainly farmland. If one approaches from the A49 at Prees Green, the parish boundary and Lower Heath area begins at the crossroads, with a straight mile ahead. At the end of the straight mile is our Lower Heath Church of England Primary School, which started out as "Industry Hall" erected in 1799 by Sir Richard Hill for the purpose of educating the children of labourers on his estate. He states: "To be instructed in reading and work of various kinds to fit them to be good and useful servants."

The boundary takes in Sandford on the A41 as far as Aychley and as the crow flies, back towards Fauls Green via Hoarstone through Mickley and Northwood. The church of Holy Immanuel was built in 1854, (and consecrated in 1856) to commemorate the coming of age of the Hon. Rowland Clegg-Hill.

The Church Hall was the gift of the Revd. Caddock Adams, (a very forward-looking vicar, since very little has had to be done to meet today's Health and Safety requirements) opened on 13th December 1938.

At Fauls, we have been very fortunate to have our very own historian in our midst; Roger West. Roger had the ability to soak up, (and remember), snippets of history and personal experiences of the older people of the parish and add them to his well-researched historical work. With Mary, his wife, in charge of his slides, Roger's talks were so passionate and entertaining. On the many occasions when he was guest speaker, often a member of the audience would remember something parents or grandparents had talked about and this was duly added to Roger's repartee. His monthly write-ups in the church magazine were usually the first words many people looked for and were especially valuable to newcomers to the wider parish of Prees.

It is good and a credit to Anne, that her father's work has been fondly and painstakingly compiled and published to take a small rural parish through this intriguing journey of more than 150 years, to learn how it has evolved and thrived to become the much-respected hub of activity it is today.

Freda Ridgway

A life-long family friend, Freda was awarded the British Empire Medal for services to the local community. (2015)

Introduction

At first glance this appears to be "The History of Lower Heath School" however, as you turn the pages it is so much more. It represents a 150-year snapshot in time of the historical and social evolution of a small parish in North Shropshire and its links to the United Kingdom and beyond.

My father has kept a diary for 53 years and has written articles for the Parish Venture magazine on local history, for over 20 years, stopping at the age of 90! He is also a prolific reader and collector of many things including books; a trait he passed on to me.

The locality of Fauls Parish sits in part of the former grand estate of the Hills of Hawkestone Park. They played a key role not only in the development of Shropshire, but of England and much further afield. Whilst this book refers to various members of the Hill family, it is devoted to the establishment and development of a local school, Lower Heath Church of England School. It blossomed into a fine institution, which continues today, from its early days as Industry Hall, built by the Hill family to educate the children of workers on their estates.

My dad's deep interest with the Hill family began at a very early age. His family home, Cumberbach House (built by Mr. Cumberbach on land purchased from the Hill's Estate) had views of Hawkestone hill from its position nestled in the remaining woodland behind the former Estate timber mill. This interest probably deepened due to his two elder brothers' steadfast refusal to include him on their adventures up to

Hawkestone: "Mam! Keep our Roger in, he will only slow us down," was the consistent response to his pleas to be included.

My grandad would distract dad by saying: "Come on Roger lets go and look for badgers and foxes down the wood," and, it would be a few years later before dad with his friend Wal Wilkinson, whose grandmother lived by Hawkestone lake, finally got to explore the grounds of Hawkestone.

Throughout his life dad collected postcards and stories of the local area, becoming the local historian. When he retired, he increased the number of talks and slide shows given to interested parties all over the county, including Women's Institutes, Church groups, Rotatory Clubs and, the Shrewsbury and Prees Historical Society' and exhibitions at Lower Heath School.

For 60 years the Hills former home was run by the Catholic Church as a spiritual retreat and dad was asked by Father McBride to attend on the first Friday of each intake to show slides of Hawkestone and the surrounding area. This amounted to 3 intakes per year, with a total of 67 shows before the Hall was sold by the Church. It allowed the attendees – requiring respite from some dire situations – to understand the history of the beautiful place where they had come to enjoy their 3-month sabbatical.

For a long time, I suggested that dad had the makings of a book and should publish. That people beyond the Parish would not only find his thoroughly researched and detailed 150-year history of the development of Lower Heath school fascinating, but also the social development of a community twisting and turning through the ages, with associated ebbs and flows of good times and challenges, including two world wars, an influx of evacuees and the government take-over of schools.

I was eventually granted the privilege of working with dad and mum, who has been a constant support in dads ventures and adventures, to have compiled and edited this book using dad's articles and photographic collection. I have retained the magazine publication dates of month and year in the body of the text as chapter headings and, whilst the compilation is largely chronological, there is a small amount of repetition usually offering a different perspective.

There is one repeating exception; with each November issue, dad devoted his article to the British Armed Forces and, it was always based on what was foremost in his mind at the time of writing.

His writing takes us up to the year 1950, 4 years after he left school in 1946.

It has been a labour of love and enabled me to gain a deeper understanding of my roots and the important contribution the little parish of Fauls Green made to the country and the wider world.

Editors' Note: some of the writing features words and descriptions associated with the vernacular of that time.

Contents

Acknowledgements   vii
Other Sources of Information   ix
Forward   xi
Introduction   xiii
Contents   xvi

Part One: The Hills and Robert Goffin

Chapter 1. April 2006: Industry Hall A Sound Foundation   3
Chapter 2. June 2006: Sir Richard Hill   6
Chapter 3. July/August 2006: Reverand Brian Hill   12
Chapter 4. Sept 2006: Hill Family Heritage   15
Chapter 5. October 2006: Lady Elizabeth Hill   20
Chapter 6. November 2006: World War II Remembered School Show 2006   23
Chapter 7. May 2008: Lady Anne Hill   28
Chapter 8. June 2008: Mr. Robert Goffin   31
Chapter 9. July/August 2008: Her Majesties Inspectorate of Schools Reports (Plus Others)   38
Chapter 10. September 2008: School Treat   41
Chapter 11. October 2008: Singing   45
Chapter 12. November 2008: 1914-1918 War   49
Chapter 13. February 2009: Goffin v Taylor   52

Part Two: Mr Robert Taylor

Chapter 14.	March 2009: Mr Robert Taylor Early Days	59
Chapter 15.	April 2009: School Management	62
Chapter 16.	May 2009: Raising Funds	65
Chapter 17.	June 2009: Sir Francis Sandford	69
Chapter 18.	July/August 2009: A Family Job	73
Chapter 19.	September 2009: Homework	76
Chapter 20.	October 2009: Discipline	78
Chapter 21.	December 2009/January 2010: Raising Funds for The Infants New Classroom	81
Chapter 22.	February 2010: Deed Of Gift from The Hill Family	86
Chapter 23.	March 2010: A Closed Shop	89
Chapter 24.	April 2010: Birds Nest	93
Chapter 25.	May 2010: Headmaster Notes v Student Memories	96
Chapter 26.	June 2010: The Pig	99
Chapter 27.	July/ August 2010: Be Kind	102
Chapter 28.	September 2010: Mrs. Sandford	105
Chapter 29.	October 2010: Miss Thomas	108
Chapter 30.	December 2010/ January 2011: New Windows	110
Chapter 31.	February 2011: Winter and Sickness	113
Chapter 32.	March 2011: Madge Hocknell	116
Chapter 33.	April 2011: Empire Day	119
Chapter 34.	May 2011: Grouping of the Standards, Waterloo	123
Chapter 35.	June 2011: Lord Hill, Commander-In-Chief of the British Army	127
Chapter 36.	July/August 2011: The Bennetts	132

Chapter 37.	September 2011: Retirement Announced	136
Chapter 38.	October 2011: "Behind every good man, there is always a good woman."	139
Chapter 39.	November 2011 published December 2011/ January 2012: The Great War	142
Chapter 40.	February 2012: Roger West, Birth	150
Chapter 41.	March 2012: Robert Taylor, Retirement	153
Chapter 42.	April 2012: Prees Hill	157
Chapter 43.	May 2012: Mr. Robert Taylor, The Final Bell Tolled	160
Chapter 44.	June 2017: The Small Holders	163

Part Three: Mr. Robert (Bert) Taylor

Chapter 45.	May 2018: Scots Pines	171
Chapter 46.	June 2018: The British Legion Shield	175
Chapter 47.	July/August 2018: Miss Annie Active	179
Chapter 48.	September 2018: Rev. Caddick Adams	182
Chapter 49.	October 2018: Oliver Dutton	186
Chapter 50.	November, 2018: The Sandford Brothers	189
Chapter 51.	December, 2018/January, 2019: Late Night Dancing	193
Chapter 52.	February, 2019: Sing	196
Chapter 53.	March, 2019: National Savings	200
Chapter 54.	April, 2019: Miss Parrie's Interview	203
Chapter 55.	May, 2019: Absent from School	206
Chapter 56.	June, 2019: Building Spree	210
Chapter 57.	July/August, 2019: Tern Hill Air Field	214
Chapter 58.	September, 2019: Everton Evacuees	218
Chapter 59.	October, 2019: Bombs Falling	222

Chapter 60.	November, 2019: Evacuees Experience	225
Chapter 61.	December, 2019/January, 2020: The Benefits of Drinking Milk	228
Chapter 62.	February, 2020: Salute the Soldiers Week	232
Chapter 63.	March, 2020: Yellow Balls of Fluff	236
Chapter 64.	September, 2020 (Published 4 months later, due to Covid-19): Eating Well	240
Chapter 65.	October, 2020: Wild Flowers	243
Chapter 66.	November, 2020: "Life on the Farm"	247
Chapter 67.	December, 2020/January, 2021: Links to Australia	251
Chapter 68.	February, 2021: Miss Gilbert	254
Chapter 69.	March, 2021: Foxes and Hounds	257
Chapter 70.	April, 2021: Road Safety and School Meals	261
Chapter 71.	May, 2021: Sandford Records Retained	265
Chapter 72.	June, 2021: Nibs and Inkwells	269
Chapter 73.	July/August, 2021: Retirement Announced	273
Chapter 74.	September, 2021: "There is always a book on the shelf to help!...."	276

PART ONE
The Hills and Robert Goffin

CHAPTER 1

April 2006: Industry Hall A Sound Foundation

I suppose, when we go sailing into the evening of our lives, the pension book safely behind the clock, plus all the other ailments that beset us, one pleasing element is our ability to reminisce. This can give lots of pleasure, that costs nothing! Having been a collector of old postcards and photographs for many years, reminiscing is second nature to me. It is most rewarding when, having lent an album to a family I get a response like, "Roger, we enjoyed your pictures so much, we did not get to bed till the early hours" or, "Can we keep your pictures a bit longer, we've got a relative coming over, who would love to see them."

On the most pleasant occasion last April (2005), we were invited by Mrs. Holland, a teacher at Lower Heath School, to talk in general about the school and its past. She agreed it would be a good idea to illustrate it with pictures, as the children would relate to a picture much better than just the spoken word.

I was a bit apprehensive about doing it but, was thrilled to bits having done it! The children came in single file, about fifty of them, and sat cross legged on the carpet, without a murmur. They showed very little reaction to the pictures. However, I was very pleasantly surprised the next day when I received 30 letters from the children, making me fully aware, that they had not missed a single thing!

The feedback was so enthusiastic and it gives me considerable pleasure to record some of it here, and to elaborate further. In a time-slot of about forty minutes, we showed 69 slides about the school, past and present and those that added a bit of humour of course, but one could only "cherry-pick" a few bits and pieces from such a rich tapestry of wonderful local history, spanning two centuries.

Some of the children expressed some surprise at the age of their school, which is one of the oldest schools in Shropshire. It was built as Industry Hall by Sir Richard Hill, who was the 2nd Baronet of Hawkestone (1733–1808) with the help of some money left by his step-mother Dame Mary Hill, who was the second wife of Sir Rowland Hill, himself the 1st Baronet of Hawkestone (1705–1783), at a cost of £230. It was built on a site two miles from Hawkstone Hall – the country seat of the Hill family – near the high road to Whitchurch, and was opened on the 6th November 1799.

The first intake of children were 30 girls and 10 boys. They were in the charge of two mistresses; Mary Bradshaw, who oversaw the establishment, and lived on the premises with her father and mother, and Hannah Blantarn who lived near to Industry Hall with a family of her own.

The school's hours were 8.00 a.m. to 5.00 p.m. in summer and 9.00 a.m. to 4.00 p.m. in winter, and six days a week with the two mistresses doing alternate days. Mary's salary was £16 per annum, with an allowance of £4 for coal and Hannah's was £12 per annum. Parents of the children were expected to pay 1s.6d. (7 1/2p in today's money) per quarter, for their education and training; but lots of families could not even afford this amount.

Industry Hall was well named. It rapidly became a hive of activity, and focal point of the community. Sir Richard Hill had done his job well, which he considered to be his public duty. He had created a much-needed tide of opportunity, to enable children to acquire the ability to read, write and put skills in their hands, and to secure for themselves, a livelihood and self-respect.

The first forty pupils were the children of the neighbouring cottages, whose parents were employed on the Estate, or in agriculture. They hardly earned enough to keep body and soul together, let alone pay 1s.6d. per quarter for their children's education. In the beginning, the children were rude and undisciplined, but the Mistresses were ordered to treat the children tenderly, and to only use the "rod" in extreme circumstances. Soon they became well behaved and orderly.

Rules were: to start at five years of age and stay for a minimum of three years with two months holiday in the year; a fortnight at Christmas, a week at Easter and Whitsuntide; a month at harvest; and two days each for the setting of and gathering of potatoes. The children were rewarded for good behaviour and attendance. Any child absent, other than for sickness, more than one day a fortnight, must signify the cause to the Mistress upon pain of forfeiting any reward due.

Industry Hall was an instant success with its schooling six days a week, and it was also used for Church services on Sundays; which were very well attended.

My thanks to the children for their most interesting letters, to which I will respond over time.

CHAPTER 2

June 2006: Sir Richard Hill

When the Rev. Edwin Sidney commenced writing his biography of Sir Richard Hill, it stretched to 533 pages with the first line being a quote from the Lord Chief Justice of England stating: "A better man I know not in the circle of human nature."

Sir Richard Hill

Sir Richard became the master of Hawkstone in 1783 – a vast estate at this time – and was also the Tory Member of

Parliament for Shropshire. In addition to building Industry Hall, he developed Hawkestone Park and in line with grand estates of that time built most of the Follies. He produced a visitor's guide to Hawkestone Park which became so popular, it necessitated the building of a place for visitors to stay called Hawkestone Inn. These Follies, defined by Oxford Dictionary as, "a costly ornamental building with no practical purpose, especially a tower of Mock-gothic ruin built in a large garden or park," still exist today as part of a pleasure walking trail owned by Hawkestone Park Hotel which sits on the original site of Hawkestone Inn. Hawkestone Park Hotel has 2 golf courses and now covers a large part of the former Hawkestone Park, that belonged to the Hill family. The golf courses facilitated the tuition of Sandy Lyle.

Gingerbread Hall (a Hawkestone Park Folly)

On the way to the Grotto (a Hawkestone Park Folly)

Edwin Sidney also mentions, "that in all essential points of character he was the model of a Christian gentleman." Well, it is a certain fact his pen, throughout those many pages, flowed with enthusiasm for Sir Richard, none more so than when relating to the building and beginnings of Lower Heath School. Yes, he conveys in no uncertain manner that the setting up of this institution was... just that bit special. So, thanks to Edwin Sidney, we know considerably more details about the early days of the school. He also mentions Rev. Brian Hill, Sir Richard's brother, who was very much involved hands-on in the early running of the school, and who also wrote a pamphlet in 1804, from which Sidney also quotes at some length.

The school business was extremely well regulated, with a pleasant mixture of lessons, the emphasis on reading to begin with, and working with their hands. The day's proceedings were always started with a prayer; all possible attention was paid to sound religious teaching, as it was considered the only safe basis of instruction at that time. The prayer was quite long, written either by Sir Richard (who wrote several hymns),

"THERE IS ALWAYS A BOOK ON THE SHELF...!"

or his brother Rev. Brian Hill, who lived on the Estate at the Citadel, Weston-under-Redcastle at this time.

The principal work done in the early days at Industry Hall, was the production of woollen goods, and the raw material was delivered in the form of fleeces. Then in what seemed to be a well organised supply line, the fleeces were picked by one group, carded by another, and spun by a third group. Finally, it was knitted into stockings or made into hearth and carriage rugs and other useful articles, such as shoes formed of cloth or matting and lined with wool. This work was supervised by Mary Bradshaw, and the girls soon became very efficient, she said "it was surprising to see the dexterity with which they handled their needles, and this work was met with considerable encouragement."

The goods, which were referred to as carriage comforts, were sold by Mr. Windsor, Haberdasher at Weston-under-Redcastle, near Hawkstone Inn, where they were eagerly purchased and thus helped to pay for the school children's education and clothing.

I was interested to note an entry in the school log book for June 12th 1986. On this day Mrs. Blower (a former Head Teacher) had organised a demonstration of the above woollen work, by Mrs. Cattell for the Class 1 children to look at and appreciate the types of lessons of the past.

Rev. Brian Hill's description of Industry Hall sums up these early beginnings stating: "Monday is the day of examination, when the children are catechised (Christian study) and rewards distributed. The names of the scholars are listed on a slate and recorded for every day's absence and, every fault. These are again noted in the black book, which is brought out on the annual festival, known as the "Big Day" among the children, when prizes were given for good behaviour, distributed according to the number of marks. The festival was held on the 1st of July, and the children and mothers were entertained with tea and rolls".

This festival appears to have been quite a spectacle, put on by the Hill family for the school, which was attended by visitors and many of their friends. It was a good way of publicising how much good might be done to society, at a small expense and, also most importantly, to set an example for their initiative.

To help support this part of the expenditure, Sir Richard took the liberty of inviting contributions from his friends and all well-wishers of the school. He also directed that collecting boxes be placed in Hawkstone Inn, and Industry Hall.

An early photograph of Hawkestone Park Hotel which was developed from Hawkestone Inn.

In the erection and management of Industry Hall, Sir Richard Hill had anticipated the need for education and instruction of that day's children. It was still far in the future, when education would become demanded and given, other than by a few wealthy men.

Sir Richard, now in his declining years, was followed by other members of the family, who continued to show considerable interest and support for the school, throughout much of the 19th century.

So, through the wastes, enclosure and turmoil of the late 18th century, the children of Industry Hall and their futures were the winners and rightly so.

CHAPTER 3

July/August 2006: Reverand Brian Hill

The foundations of Industry Hall (latterly Lower Heath School), were well and truly laid in 1799, so much so, that today it is still a busy thriving school with a headmistress in charge, just as it started 207 years ago. Probably with little change, other than dress, and most of the children being conveyed to school on their own feet in the past.

Of course, for the early years, the school was principally supported by the Hills of Hawkstone, who each in their turn were more determined that Industry Hall would be a success. Early accounts show us that the expense of running the establishment for the first five years, was about £50 per year. This included the purchase of clothing for the children with coats, waistcoats, breeches and straw hats for the boys, and linsey gowns, handkerchiefs, and bonnets for the girls.

This fascinating detail comes from the pen of the Rev. Brian Hill, who as previously mentioned, seemed to be very involved in the welfare and running of the school. At this time, he was probably Chaplain to the Hill family, preceding Rev. Bolland and Rev. Bagshaw.

His pamphlet of 1804 has been frequently quoted from in the past, but recently an earlier one was found in the Shropshire Archives written by him in 1801. This was similar to the one of 1804, but he also mentions their July Festival of 1801 whilst describing with names, the prize money given to children. For this festival £8.0s.3/4d. had been raised through

"THERE IS ALWAYS A BOOK ON THE SHELF...!"

the charity boxes at Industry Hall and Hawkstone Inn, in each box a small amount of silver and gold had been placed, plus there were donations from friends and well-wishers of the school.

This money was distributed in prize money for spinners, knitters, good behaviour, and attendance. Even the five out of forty who did not qualify, were given a little prize, preventing any sad countenances appearing on the Festival Day. The names of the spinners and knitters were written on slips of paper and sealed up and fixed to their work. The ladies present, having examined the work, gave their judgement and the prizes were awarded accordingly.

Out of the six spinners, Sarah Reynolds, who was eleven years old, won the first prize for both spinning and knitting, with Mary Abbotts, aged ten, coming second and Elizabeth Ridgway also ten, coming third. Out of a total of fourteen knitters Sarah Husbands, aged eleven came second, with Eleanor Turner aged nine, coming third.

Hill also mentions six readers of which three, won awards. Anne Blantarn, the daughter of the mistress, aged eight, was the winner with Mary and Anne Ridgway coming second and third.

Prizes for good behaviour and regular attendance seemed to go together and was tied between four children, John Sherwood, Thomas Hudson, Maria, and Elizabeth Ridgway.

Five shillings were given to Thomas Jones, a very deserving boy and upon leaving the school, he went to live with an uncle in Birmingham.

The remaining sum of £1.12s.8 1/2d. was laid out on entertainment and the provision of food.

Yes, Rev. Brian Hill, of the Citadel, certainly gives a wonderful insight into the workings of Lower Heath School, 205 years ago. He emphasised in these accounts, "that the expenditure has been detailed, for the satisfaction of those benevolent friends of Industry Hall, who have had the goodness to contribute to the festival, and hopes they are satisfied that considerable pains have been taken, to bestow their bounty, in a just and impartial manner." He also hoped it would encourage others to support the school and its manufacture.

The Citadel on Hills Estate

Rev. Brian Hill also mentions Mrs. Bull, who was resident head mistress in 1801, she not only confined herself as superintendent of the school, but she also employed her skills in making a good savoury soup for the neighbouring poor. This was sold at 1/2d. a quart, and made twice a week, forty quarts at a time. Sir Richard Hill would send two large loaves of bread to be distributed in equal portions at each making; the poor had thereby obtained some comfortable meals.

Yes, not a lot of change generally, but thankfully this part of the past, the provision of soup and bread, is no longer relevant.

CHAPTER 4

Sept 2006: Hill Family Heritage

The recent 150th celebrations of Fauls Church, (2006), gave lots of parishioners of all ages, the opportunity to dig deep and produce, with their talents, a festival for several hundred people; a feast to behold. The combination of church and school, did our little parish proud, with floral displays in the church, re-enactment of the school history in the church hall, plus ample wholesome food.

Of the many and varied exhibits for the discerning eye on which to tarry, I particularly enjoyed the 150 potted flowers either side of the tarmac path, depicting the 150 years, put there by the children of Lower Heath School. Likewise pots of flowers were placed on an adjacent grave, that of Maria Naylor, one of the schoolgirl's initial mistresses, who died before her time in 1873.

A Hill family crest hung from the balcony, painstakingly done in coloured fabrics, of which the Hill family would have been proud.

Hill Family Crest (2006)

They certainly left us a wonderful heritage with our school, church and in many other ways. All that gives me an excuse to ponder, a little more in depth, about various members of the Hill family, especially those who participated in the creating of our heritage. I suppose one could say, the fabric of our parish originated from 1787, on the death of Dame Mary Hill.

She had been the second wife of Sir Rowland Hill 1st Baronet and it was money from her Estate that helped Sir Richard Hill 2nd Baronet, her stepson, to build Industry Hall in 1799. Dame Mary also left money for the building of schools at Hadnall and Weston-under-Redcastle. In fact, she left all her money to charitable causes, of which Industry Hall also had an annual payment of £10, so her heart was in the right place.

Weston-under-Redcastle School of Black and White Construction

Likewise, the Rev. Brian Hill, brother of Sir Richard, does not get a lot of mention in general, but he was certainly very instrumental in helping Industry Hall get off to a good start in the early years of the 19th century. I liked the way he encouraged, persuaded, even begged, people to subscribe to the welfare of the school. His efforts so much so contributed to creating a foundation where the school was able to expand several times throughout the 19th century, to cater for the education of the increasing number of children.

Edwin Sidney described Rev. Brian Hill as a, "man of elegant mind and engaging manners," who lived at the Citadel, Weston-under-Redcastle. Reginald Heber, Rector of Hodnet, who in 1823 became the Bishop of Calcutta, was his neighbour and close friend. Whenever Reginald had written anything new (he was a prolific hymn writer), he would carry it to Weston-under-Redcastle, where he was welcome at all hours and would read it to Rev. Brian Hill, whose literary judgement he had a high regard for. He loved the gentleness of Brian's disposition, which put him at perfect ease to accept suggested changes, if any.

In front of me, I have a Charities Commissioners Report dated 1824, which states: "There is a school and school house at Lower Heath called Industry Hall, which was established by the Hawkstone family. It is under the management of Mrs. Elizabeth Hill of the Citadel, Hawkstone, at whose expense it is principally supported."

Mrs. Elizabeth Hill, now a widow, was the daughter-in-law of Sir John Hill (1740 to 1824), who was the 3rd Baronet and on his death in 1824, Mrs. Hill's son Rowland, became the 4th Baronet following on from his grandfather. It was this Sir Rowland who later became the 2nd Viscount who, being persuaded by Archdeacon Allen, for local George Robinson's, "idea of a church at Fauls", made it become a reality; to celebrate his son's majority. Hence, our beautiful little church at Fauls Green, now in its 150th anniversary, with all the joyful celebrations mentioned above was born.

Fauls Green Church Under Construction

Fauls Green Church Viewed from the Vicarage Side

"THERE IS ALWAYS A BOOK ON THE SHELF...!"

Mrs. Elizabeth Hill who came from Exeter, married Colonel John Hill, the eldest son of Sir John Hill in 1795, four years before the building of Industry Hall. Her husband John had been an excellent manager of Hawkstone Estates, unlike his father who had previously squandered a fortune on politics. So, it was a very sad day for the family, when John died so young of flu in 1814, thus the title passing directly to his son Rowland.

Elizabeth never married again; she devoted her time to the raising of her several children and as previously mentioned, to managing and financing Lower Heath School.

CHAPTER 5

October 2006: Lady Elizabeth Hill

It is a certain fact, the original Industry Hall had done everything and much more, for the local children from quite a large catchment area. Over the first forty years, the class numbers had gone up from forty to well over a hundred, yet in the same confined space of 27ft. x 16ft., with a ceiling height of about 8ft. A gallery had been fitted along the west wall to cram the children in, but even so, it must have felt like "sardines in a tin."

The working conditions for pupils and teachers would have been very difficult, both deserving considerable credit for their attendance and perseverance. But within a few years, this was all to change. The teaching area was to be trebled, allowing boys and girls to have separate classrooms and the original Industry Hall became the infant's classroom.

I quite like this period in the progress of Lower Heath School, when the need for expansion and change became desperate. For me it is the story of two ladies of the Hill family. Elizabeth of the Citadel, who managed and financed the school, and her daughter-in-law Anne, who had married her son Rowland in 1830, and was eventually to take over the management of the school. They were two, good committed ladies to the cause, with just one important difference. Elizabeth had to manage on a shoe string, but Anne was a very wealthy young lady and she was to go on and manage the school for over forty years. So much so, it became known colloquially as Lady (Anne) Hill's School Lower Heath.

"THERE IS ALWAYS A BOOK ON THE SHELF...!"

However, in passing, I think Elizabeth deserves more of a mention. She would have become the leading lady of the Hill family on the death of her mother-in-law in 1806, having married her eldest son John in 1795.

She was widowed in 1814 with several children, plus the death of Sir Robert Hill in 1808, (builder of the school), meant life could not have been easy for her in managing the school, with its big increase in numbers, and a limited budget. I suppose Elizabeth's budget was a sign of the times, as the Estate was going through difficulties, not helped by her father-in-law, Sir John Hill, squandering a small fortune on politics. There was also the problem of the country being at War with Napoleon in the Peninsula, culminating in the Battle of Waterloo, the last of 15 battles against the French.

Sir John, who was a prolific producer of children, emphasised to them "he'd got no money" other than for their education, hence, five of his sons joined the Army. So, Elizabeth had got lots of brothers-in-law to turn to for advice, but it was Rowland, Sir John's eldest son, after Colonel John her husband died, who she would correspond with for advice on various matters.

And it was this Rowland Hill (1772 to 1842) who became a famous General during the Napoleonic wars. In 1828 he became Commander in Chief of the British Army, and being so admired by his men, was known as "Daddy Hill". He also became the 1st Viscount Hill. He never married, dying without issue which led to Elizabeths son becoming the 2nd Viscount.

I have read some of Elizabeth's correspondence and she comes over as a caring, concerned person. So, it must have been of great satisfaction to her, to see Anne, her daughter-in-law, take over the managing of the school and more importantly the financing, and to put in motion all the improvements she was not able to do.

She died in 1842, the year that her eldest son Rowland, became the 2nd Viscount. Another son John, was to become Curate at Weston-under-Redcastle where he remained for over 60 years.

Anne's name was to become synonymous with Lower Heath School. By now, the name Industry Hall, and its manufacture had gone, and in the first Log Book it was referred to as Viscountess Hill's School, Lower Heath.

One gets a different impression of Anne, to Elizabeth. Well, you would step out of line, at your peril, with Anne, but at the same time she had an endearing quality. In other words, she was very firm, but fair.

She came from hard-bitten stock, as her family, the Clegges, had made a fortune out of manufacturing in Lancashire. She was only sixteen when she married into the Hill family and became its leading lady in 1830, moving to Hawkestone Hall. Even so, I am sure she was to benefit by having Elizabeth around for her first few years.

Hawkestone Hall Front Elevation

CHAPTER 6

November 2006: World War II Remembered – School Show

Earlier this year (2006), the children at Lower Heath School were doing a project on World War II, with the emphasis on local contributions and how events affected the school. On Monday January 23rd, several people were invited by their teachers, to help the children with their recollections and memories, of which I was privileged to be one of them. It proved to be a most rewarding afternoon, albeit, a little daunting. The teachers and children were certainly up for it, with ample measures of enthusiasm and preparation to concentrate our thinking and disperse the cobwebs.

The main avenues to pursue, were the

- development of Prees Heath as an Airfield for first, the training of bomber crews, and then the glider crews;
- people who were called up for active service;
- all the many local services, who were said "kept the home fires burning;"
- and various intakes of evacuees, who came by train from Liverpool, to escape the bombing.

Mr. Bill Ashley with a life time's experience of fighting fires, gave an interesting talk on all the various pumps and systems deployed. He also mentioned his Army service as a tank driver with the Guards Armoured Division on the Continent. At this point, a young pupil asked him, if he had ever met Mr. Hitler, to which Bill replied with some hesitation, "that he had not exactly met Mr. Hitler, but he had met some of his friends, and they were not very pleasant."

Mr. Bill Ashley Dressed in his Fire Tunic taken earlier in his life. (Mr. Green LH side and Charlie Price RH side of photo)

Mrs. Sylvester talked about the scarcity of food during the War and how we were all rationed. She then demonstrated the exact measured quantities of food, people were entitled to for just one week, which created a lot of interest and amazement.

Our contribution (my wife Mary and I), was to show the children 36 slide pictures, previously selected by the teacher, Mrs. Holland. Most of these pictures illustrated Sir Alfred McAlpine's' creation of the Airfield at Prees Heath, which was opened on August 1st, 1942.

Whilst most of the buildings have long since been demolished, a few relics of the past remain. These include the four Aircraft

"THERE IS ALWAYS A BOOK ON THE SHELF...!"

Hangers, Officer's Mess, Underground Command Post – thankfully never needed – and the Control Tower: wouldn't it be nice to see that restored to its former glory? **

Photographs of other buildings, now gone, especially aerial images of the three 150ft. wide landing strips, still clearly discernible, taken some years ago by Paul Jackson, doing a project for his A-levels, with the kind help of Ray Grocott.

Throughout World War II, I was at Lower Heath School and remember well the Whitley Bombers, flying over the playground on their round the clock circuit and bumps, and later, the Sterling Bombers towing Horsa Gliders. But, by far the saddest event, was the Wellington bomber crash landing adjacent to the school, killing the five members of the crew. I am sure the pilot, who was only twenty-one, brought his plane down, which was on fire, on an angle, missing the properties of Rookery Cottages, Woodside and to the right of Cover Side. It was a very sad lesson to see the 60ft. R.A.F. transporter removing the mangled wreckage a few days later.

Local people who had gone to Lower Heath School were involved in active service at Dunkirk, North Africa, the Normandy landings, and the Far East and various other parts of the world.

The first one to be called up was George Mellor. George, who was in the Militia (Home Guard), was notified of his call up by the police arriving at his work place! After being evacuated from Dunkirk, he was posted with the Royal Artillery to North Africa, where he was taken prisoner. We were happy to show pictures of George and his gun crew, in the desert of North Africa, plus the many faces of people who contributed through service in the Fire Service, Civil Defence, Observer Corps, Home Guard etc.

Fauls Green Home Guard

Home Guard on Armistice Day Parade (Prees Church)

The first intake of evacuees from Liverpool arrived, all carrying their gas masks, on September 2nd 1939, a day before War was declared, arrangements having been made months earlier. A second intake arrived the day before Christmas Eve, with a third one later, which created an over flow, and these were accommodated in the Hall at Fauls.

Thankfully, now safe from the German bombing of Liverpool, although we did have one local scare.

"THERE IS ALWAYS A BOOK ON THE SHELF...!"

German bombers were regularly heard over Fauls Parish, and on the 28th November 1940, a stick of bombs fell within a short distance of the school. Three of them fell in Lower Heath Woods and one over the road in the gateway of Mr. Johnson's meadow, who on arriving next morning with his few cows said, "Of all the places to drop a bomb Why! Oh Why! Bang in the middle of a gateway." The next day lots of people came to view the hole and collect the shrapnel.

Although it was a traumatic time for evacuees and their teachers, they soon adapted to country life and I am sure we all benefited from their presence and lots of long-term relationships were forged.

I love the story of the two Henderson boys, Jimmy, and Ronnie, who were welcomed as a family, at the Darliston home of the Wilkinson family. Wallace Wilkinson told me that on the day following their arrival (Christmas Eve) his mother sent him on the Salopian bus to Whitchurch to purchase all the necessary requisites to make their Christmas as good as possible. Today, over half a century later, they, the evacuees still visit that cottage.

For the last few minutes, we split up into groups, where Mrs. Haycocks talked about evacuees, Mrs. Ridgeway talked about the Land Army and Mrs. Turner about the Navy, Army and Air Forces Institutes and she had a good question to field... how many slices were there in a Swiss Roll?

** **Editors Note:** Since dad wrote this article the Control Tower was restored in 2014 by the Butterfly Conservation charity following receipt of a Heritage Lottery grant. It is now a refuge for birds, bats, and hibernating butterflies and moths. External panels on the building also tell the story of its history.

CHAPTER 7
May 2008: Lady Anne Hill

As mentioned in 1838, Lady Anne Hill of Hawkstone had quietly taken over the running of Lower Heath School from her mother-in-law Elizabeth, who lived at the Citadel at Weston-under-Redcastle. Anne who was to become a Viscountess in 1842, the year Elizabeth died, tackled the job with considerable relish and enthusiasm for her young years; she was just 24.

One of her priorities was to build a new Master's house extension on the old Industry Hall and employ Robert Goffin as Headmaster at a salary of £70 per year. Robert Goffin, then aged 19, was born in Great Yarmouth. He came to Whitmore station in Staffordshire, the nearest station in that day. Hearsay tells us, a broad-shouldered youth pushed all his worldly goods on a wheel barrow all the 16 miles to Lower Heath School for 2s. 6d. (12 1/2p today). Be as it may, Robert, who never married, devoted all his working life to teaching at Lower Heath School, retiring after 37 years. He was not a certificated teacher.

So, seemingly with old heads on young shoulders and of course with willing helpers, a most pressing requirement for Lady Anne Hill and her management team, was more space. The Old Industry Hall with its 30 girls and 10 boys had now become over a 100 and was still growing. A large classroom extension was built on the garden to the rear, measuring 65ft. x 20ft. and it must have been a state-of-the-art classroom, for that day. It was a two-storey building, open to the rafters,

"THERE IS ALWAYS A BOOK ON THE SHELF...!"

full length sash windows and a bell turret on the gable. The classroom was split in two with a curtain partition, boys, and girls either side; the boys' side was 10ft. bigger with a tiered gallery.

There was some discussion as to where the stores would be positioned, and Lord Hill, on one of his few visits, Anne usually did the visiting, decreed that they would go in the centre of each classroom... Later they were moved to the side. Oh! And every Sunday morning the curtain partition would be removed, the desks repositioned to face the front, and the Rev. Bagshaw, Lord Hill's chaplain, would come down from Hawkstone Hall, through the North Lodge in his horse and trap, to take a church service, which were very well attended.

A century on (1938), I sat in those classrooms, now mixed, and much more fun. Now, one hundred and sixty years on; thankfully children are still sitting in that class, part of which is now the hall. As of 2008 the school – including its time as Industry Hall – has now been in existence for 209 years.

On the 8th January 1872, the Headmaster Robert Goffin started the first Lower Heath School Log Book. In a beautiful copperplate hand, he wrote:

VISCOUNTESS HILLS (CHURCH OF ENGLAND) SCHOOL, LOWER HEATH.

He went on to make 192 entries before his retirement on August 2nd 1875, when the school was put under new management. One is inclined to think what a shame, his first 34 years commencing in 1838 and not a record. Still, what he recorded is a wonderful intimate detail of how the school functioned (assuming earlier hypothetical entries of a similar nature) through the middle part of the 19th century.

Lower Heath School Front Elevation (20th Century)

CHAPTER 8

June 2008: Mr. Robert Goffin

Although, we only have records for the last 2 years and 8 months of Robert Goffin's 37 years Headship of Lower Heath School, one can delve elsewhere, such as the Church Records, history of the Hill family and other local documents, to assess the character and wellbeing of the man. That he was a big success is without doubt, and seemingly with the patience of Job.

Well, I suppose every necessary ingredient was nicely dovetailed in for a young 19-year-old Robert Goffin. That he took advantage and excelled himself was very much to his credit, even though he had a lady for a boss, very unusual for that day, and a Viscountess as well, who regularly visited the school. Of the 79 recorded visitations, 29 were by Lady Hill.

Lady Anne would often bring a relative or friend to examine the children in their lessons and was always full of encouragement for them. Of course, this adds up to hundreds of visits by her Ladyship during their parallel association with the school and it is no wonder she built her own private road to the school named Coach Drive, lined with trees, rhododendrons, and paved entrances; to avoid paying tolls.

Coach Drive Approach to School

Other visitors were the Vicar, who usually expressed satisfaction at the answers to his questions and his wife being full of praise for the girls work with their sewing. HMIS, formed in 1839, and for Lower Heath this was a former Sergeant Major. He would call in and take the children for drill, which was very popular. There were various other visitors and they all, as you might say, looked over Robert Goffin's shoulder. In his 2 years and eight months of log book entries there are only seven weeks, when he wrote "No visitors".

One of Robert Goffin's specialties seems to have been, well it certainly arrests my attention, that he loved to get those children singing. He had made lists of two dozen songs he had taught them, several about the sea, as he came from the seaside and others that caught my eye were: "Happy days for Childhood," "Oh! The Sports of Childhood" and "Secretly the Bells are Ringing."

"THERE IS ALWAYS A BOOK ON THE SHELF...!"

One (journalist's) recorded occasion in 1854 caught my eye: "Great Rejoicings at Lower Heath – The Oaklands Broadhay," where Sir Rowland Hill had an extensive timber mill, employing a great number of workmen.

Lower Heath Timber Yard 1900

Inside Hills Estate Timber Yard

The workmen with their wives, sweethearts, and school children congregated in the yard to celebrate the majority of Rowland (Clegg-Hill), the Hawkstone Heir. The workshop became the ballroom, tastefully decorated with evergreens. Dinner and tea were served, very nice and in abundance. A portion of the North Shropshire Cavalry Band was in attendance. A very beautiful maypole was erected and alongside it, triumphal arches. The scene was all set for the children from Lady Anne's School, under the direction of Mr. Goffin, the Master of that excellent institution to start the entertainment of dancing and singing.

The most gratifying event of the occasion wrote the journalist, was the singing of a special song for the Hawkstone Heir, which went like this:

> "With joy we raise our notes on high
> In mirth and glee our parts to bear;
> With merry hearts our wishes sing,
> Good health, long life to Hawkstone's Heir.
>
> We wish him richly blest on earth,
> That honoured, loved and free from care;
> In this fair place which gave him birth,
> He long may live the Hawkstone Heir.
>
> May God on him his blessings pour,
> His soul for fairer scenes prepare;
> That when his earthly course is o'er,
> In heaven may you live the Hawkstone Heir.
>
> The Lord his parents bless we pray,
> Who love the poor their gifts to share;
> Long may he live to bless this day,
> When first drew breath the Hawkstone Heir."

The Oakland's, is now the home of the Ridgeway family and would have been one of the earliest building conversions done by Mr. Faulkner in the late 1930's, a retired businessman who used to ride a bike and keep pigeons for a hobby.

Ridgeways Family House on the site of Hills Estate Timber Yard

It is a certain fact their singing was much appreciated by V.I.P.'s from far and wide, when on the 29th May 1856, they sang for the dedication service of Fauls Church. I am glad there was a visiting journalist there, who wrote: "The choir of Viscountess Hill's School, Lower Heath, under the direction of their Master Mr. Goffin, chanted the 'Venite Te Deum' and 'Jubilate' then sang the 84th and Old Hundredth Psalms, in very creditable style, near raising the roof, accompanied by a harmonium."

The congregation included the bishop and 36 robed Vicars. So, it was "well done Robert Goffin."

Fauls Green Church Opening Day 1857

But one very important happening in May 1857, recorded by the Vicar of Fauls, concentrated local thinking. With only a few hours' notice, subscription (money) was raised to greet the return of Sir Rowland and Lady Anne Hill to Hawkstone, whose absence had been prolonged by the "serious illness of her Ladyship; her health now much improved." The venue was Marchamley Lodge, an entrance to the park, where a beautiful arch festooned with flowers was erected.

Marchamley Lodge

"THERE IS ALWAYS A BOOK ON THE SHELF...!"

The children from Lower Heath School numbering 200 (smaller ones on horse and wagon), under the charge of Miss. Naylor, Miss. Thomason, and Mr. Goffin, preceded by a banner, "Welcome Home", walked to Marchamley singing all the way and determined to enjoy themselves. Here they met up with 80 children from Marchamley School, and their banner read "Long live our Patroness", and who were equally "qui vive".

On arriving at the Lodge, they formed on the green in double rows to receive their noble patrons. After the carriage had passed, they all set about doing justice to the well laden tables of food. The children then entertained the large gathered throng, with their amusing school songs, concluding with the National Anthem. The day's proceedings were ended by several races for the boys, who competed for the balance of the subscription money, after which they quietly dispersed to their homes.

Yes! Concentrated thoughts. Replaced with rejoicing for Anne, her Ladyships' "return to health." I doubt the tiredness in all those little legs was noticed, bundled with all the excitement and memory forming activities of the day, as they retraced their steps, homeward bound.

CHAPTER 9

July/ August 2008: Her Majesties Inspectorate of Schools Reports (Plus Others)

During the final years of Robert Goffin's 37 years as Headmaster of Lower Heath School, a very important happening was taking place, and this would benefit the school and all schools.

With the coincidence of the declining fortunes of the Hill family, who had carried the burden of its expense for the first 75 years, government grants were now being made available. This resulted in the visitation of HMIS to assess the teaching qualities of the school, whereby the amount of grant was fixed, less a reduction for teachers who were not certificated.

The first recorded visit of HMIS to Lower Heath was on March 26th, 1872. This was in Robert Goffin's 34th year as Master at the school and the education return stated: "Robert Goffin, Headteacher, 52 scholars; Emily Hall, Infant's teacher, 54 scholars, none of them certificated." Eventually Emily Hall, was the first to obtain a certificate at Lower Heath School; which stated, that she must have "exclusive management of the Infants, to qualify for the extra grant."

All in all, every report sent to Viscountess Hill was very favourable. But in most of those reports, singing was mentioned: "great and successful pains have been taken with singing," "the singing is very good" 1872, "the singing is exceedingly good"

"THERE IS ALWAYS A BOOK ON THE SHELF...!"

1874 and, "this school has passed a highly successful examination" 1875. Likewise, an early report of HMIS states: "The children are cheerful in their manner, clean in their appearance and neat in their dress. The examination in the elementary subjects has been thoroughly successful. The work throughout the school deserves high praise. The infants are also well cared for."

In all, Robert experienced four of these visits, plus others from the Diocesan Inspectorate and the Bible Society, when the upper class from Marchamley would attend, making the number of visits over 200.

I am sure Lady Anne would have had considerable satisfaction, in delivering these Reports to Robert Goffin as he, and his two school mistresses, would have had in receiving them. It was even more remarkable as one inspector pointed out, that if there was one defect, it came with the, "unwieldy dimensions" of the classes, which on occasions held upwards of 200 children.

Following this Report on 1854, Viscountess Hill, and her management team, decided to put another extension on the front of the Old Industry Hall. This was single storey, with a flat roof to accommodate the ever-increasing number of infants attending the school and was the last extension on the school whilst under the influence of the Hill family. **

One hundred and fifty-four years on (2008), if viewing the school from the road, the masonry is still the same, the original Industry Hall with the Mistresses' house on the right-hand side, with the Master's on the left-hand side, easily discernible by a straight line in the brickwork. What better memory could a family have of their input to a local institution?

Interestingly, during renovation of the above extension in 1992, a piece of floorboard was found with names of the estate tradesmen, architect and school teachers and it was dated 21st of June, 1854. We can certainly identify Thomas Rogers, his son John and nephew John Downing. Thomas Rogers was a master carpenter who did the beautiful decorative carved gable boards on the Hawkstone Lodges and Park House and other work of a specialist nature. He was also an enthusiastic Methodist preacher. His son John, married the builder's daughter from Prees (Mr. Powell) and became a partner in the firm.

Now back to Robert Goffin, I enjoyed his log book entry of 21st June, 1875. Viscountess Hill kindly allowed the school a holiday this day, as the teachers and many of the children were desirous of availing themselves of the opportunity of visiting Southport, "by excursion train.'

Robert Goffin and Class 2

** **Editor's Note** Today this is the library.

CHAPTER 10

September 2008: School Treat

Change, as they say, is forever with us. Change certainly came in abundance to Lower Heath School, with the death of the 2nd Viscount Hill (Sir Rowland Hill) on the 3rd January, 1875. He and mostly his wife, Viscountess Anne, had been patrons/managers and had been wholly supportive of the school for upwards of forty years. Robert Goffin, the Headmaster for most of that time, wrote of the teachers, parents, and children's desire, "to express their heart felt gratitude and unfeigned regret for the loss sustained by his death." In fact, it was the end of a very successful and, one of the most productive eras in the history of the school and the end of the Hills family association with the school.

Later that year, on the 12th August 1875, Robert Goffin made his last entry in the log book. A public meeting was held, the Rev. J.B. Lennard presiding, when, to mark the respect and esteem of their friends, parents and neighbours, the teachers were each presented with a handsome Testimonial on resigning the charge of their schools. I am sure the above meeting was very crowded and a very emotional affair. Robert Goffin and his staff had been very, very popular.

A young Robert Goffin, who would have come with recommendation, under the auspices of Lady Anne, had arrived 37 years earlier and he had weaved his "particular magic" into the heart and souls of the community. Yes, the instant chemistry of these two people – she was only a youngster too – provided a wonderful atmosphere that took the school nearly 40 years down the track, to the considerable benefit of hundreds of local children.

Hence, I use the word magic, even at a distance it bubbles through every document at my disposal.

Robert Goffin did not appear to be a disciplinarian and yet there was discipline. In all his log book entries, never did he write any anguished word or mention of punishment, other than on one occasion to do with some boys acting improperly to persons, this was, "on the way to school and returning." Their punishment was a lecture to the whole school by Lord Hill's Chaplain, Rev. Bagshaw.

All of Robert Goffin's reports by HMIS were of good quality often saying, before they left the premises, "the report will be a good one and a grant to match." They were also very impressed with the singing of the school. This very much was Robert Goffin's way he loved to get those children singing – this was his specialty. Perhaps his thinking was, "children who sing are more inclined to be happier and better behaved." I ponder! I wonder whether examiners ever listen to children sing today?

On August 10th, 1875 the Dowager Viscountess Hill (Anne) made her last of hundreds of visits to Lower Heath School in her capacity as Patron of the School. Often, she would have a visitor to the Hall with her and would take an active part in the work of the standards. She loved to listen to the children read and inspect their writing. Every Christmas, forty of the older children would write letters which would be submitted to Viscount and Viscountess Hill for their inspection. But, on this occasion, although in mourning, was to tell the children they must understand that her promised treat was not forgotten by her, seemingly with her problems, it had to be arranged for a later date.

"THERE IS ALWAYS A BOOK ON THE SHELF...!"

It was typical of Viscountess Anne with her character and years of commitment to the school – no way would she let those children down. Of course, this treat was special in as much it was to be the last treat and get together under Robert Goffin and Lady Hill, who started together and finished together.

So, the final curtain must have been a wonderful, memorable occasion for about 170 children at this time, (regardless of their circumstances) for the "many farewells" to be registered. Well! The journey, walking with horse draw wagons for the younger children, through Lady Hills Coach Drive (now obsolete) the North Lodge, on a century's old road, the most picturesque approach to Hawkstone Hills and its beautiful Georgian Mansion, but now long since covered in pasture, their destination.

Yes, a wonderful setting, complemented with all things guaranteed to make 170 Children happy, joyful, and merry.

Also, to sing their hearts out for (the last time) their now retired Headmaster, Robert Goffin, and Lady Hill (Anne) their Patron's now retired, surely an occasion for many a tear-stained cheek. George Thomas was four when the above treat took place. He lived to be 90 years plus and forever his main topic of conversation was the days of the Estate and Lord and Lady Hill.

A Mr. Salmons of Nantwich (200 years ago) put it like this: –

> "Near Hawkstone Park I'd pitch my tent,
> Near Hawkstone scenery dwell,
> In various landscapes would frequent,
> Its various beauties tell.
> For in those groves and vales I find,
> That richest jewel 'Peace of Mind'
> And Paradise below."

Hawkestone Park
View to the Valley between Lions Hill and Grotto Hill

CHAPTER 11
October 2008: Singing

I have now completed my fourth year of being invited to write for the Venture about local history, usually about the Church or School but also local life in general. It is a very pleasing process, of observing and becoming involved with people who in their day, helped to weave the fabric of our past, adding to the welfare of others as they encompassed their stage and time, in our little parish of Fauls.

For me, 1875 becomes a watershed, or a cross roads, of past, present, and future. However, I feel so reluctant to move on at this point, without more mention of the two people who so galvanised our School and applied the necessary extra foundation blocks for the two Robert Taylors, (father and son) to take it through the next three quarters of a century – Viscountess Anne Hill and Robert Goffin, Schoolmaster.

I am inclined to think – yes, I know Anne's wealth was a big factor but, the background and community atmosphere into which they were pitched, must have influenced them in the delicate art of management and teaching to which they both excelled, at their young ages of twenty-five and nineteen, which was now finished. It was now left to Mrs. Sarah Sandford (nee Halstead) – the Sandford family took over the oversight role – to follow in Anne's shoes.

By now the Hill family fortunes were poised, ready for a free fall, from which they would never recover. It must have been a very sad time for Anne, who had arrived forty-two years earlier, bringing her family's considerable wealth in her marriage to the Second Viscount at the age of sixteen. Her maiden name was Clegg and her family decreed any male children born to her, must have their name Clegg in front of Hill; hence Clegg-Hill is now the family name. I suppose they thought, having come from humble beginnings, to have a Viscountess in their family was a reward for their wealth made through the cotton industry in Lancashire. Anyway, Anne was well deserving of her title, she was patron to four other schools and seemingly devoted her life to the education of children, although it was well known, Lower Heath School was her favourite.

So, Viscountess Anne, now Dowager, having lost her husband early in 1875, her days at Hawkstone were numbered. She had also lost her daughter-in-law the year before, and her son was in the process of marrying his second wife, which took place on the 29th April, 1875. To the best of my knowledge, the very last time she was mentioned before she left for Brighton, never to return, was on the 9th August 1876, when the new headmaster of Lower Heath School, Robert Taylor wrote in the log book, "The Dowager Viscountess Hill visited the school and heard the children sing".

When a young Robert Goffin arrived as headmaster of Lower Heath School in 1839, where he lived 'over the shop', he would have immediately become aware that all roads and footpaths led to Lower Heath, creating a non-stop hive of activity. His school, where pupil numbers fluctuated between 150-200, was also used for many other occasions, business and social, in the evenings and weekends. There was always a church service on Sundays, which was very well attended, Lord Hill's Chaplain taking afternoon services, which continued in Fauls Church after it was built and consecrated in 1856.

"THERE IS ALWAYS A BOOK ON THE SHELF...!"

He would certainly have been familiar with the activities taking place on the fields around the crossroads at the Tumps (the local name given for where Lady Hills coach drive ended just before the school). Here, open air services and camp meetings were held by groups of various religious persuasion. The field adjacent to the school was where the Wesleyans and Baptists congregated, the other side of the road the Methodists, where properties are called Chapel fields, and the Salvation Army. The tollgate was situated about a hundred yards from the school, with the Baptists dipping well just over the hedge from it.

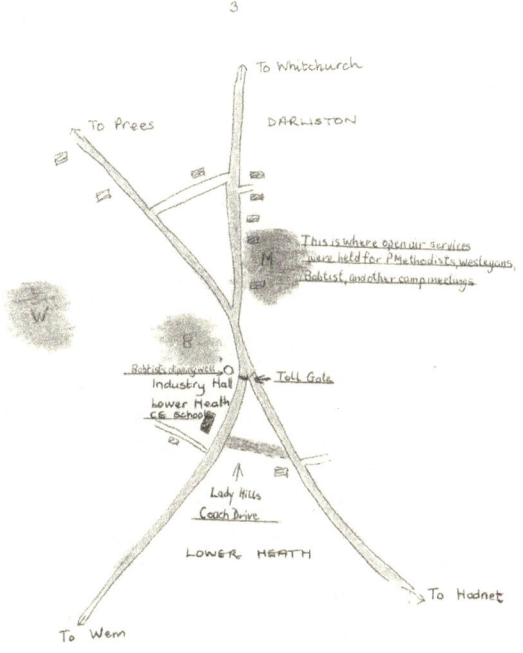

A Map Showing the Position of Industry Hall on the Hills Estate in 1835

Miss Thomas' – a local lady I got to know well – family had lived adjacent to Lower Heath School, back into the 18th century and, she was born in the Toll House. She was very much an authority on local history, which she so willingly imparted to me. When she passed away, her family kindly gave me all her notes, her notes were scribbled on the pages of an exercise book from which I will sometimes quote.

I strongly get the impression that at least one of Lady Hill's last wishes, before her departure from Shropshire, was to hear the children of her school sing yet again. Robert Goffin was an excellent teacher, an all-round teacher, but his specialty was to get his children singing. My mother said, "Singing brings much of what the soul desires."

I will now pass on from a period in the middle of the 18th century, that so arrested my attention, with a thought for today 132 years on: that Lady Hill and Robert Goffin, would have recognised that quality of life they so pursued for their scholars, so manifest in the young Headteacher of today Cathy Rutherford (Oct 2008).

CHAPTER 12
November 2008: 1914-1918 War

I have attended Fauls church all my life, having been christened there, through Sunday School, and now long past my biblical sell by date. Sitting there, I have forever been aware of the beautifully carved honours board that bears the names of the 26 men and boys – who gave their all – in defence of our Country, out of eighty-one, who served from our little Parish of Fauls, during the Great War of 1914-1918. Very nearly every family was associated to some degree with someone who never returned, but the concentration of sadness and grief encompassed everyone, and still lingers today.

Robert Taylor now in his 40th year as headmaster of Lower Heath School, had taught most of them as children. His own son had served as well but he never once mentioned the War in the school log book. However, the Rev. Harold Burton who had, by now, been Vicar of Fauls for over 30 years, gives a vivid insight into how the Parish positively responded. On one occasion he wrote: "The War was brought near to us yesterday, when Richard James Webb was laid to rest in Fauls churchyard with full military honours. The service was very impressive and reminded us all how very urgently our prayers were needed for those who are fighting by land, by water and by air, but also for all of those who, by the loss of those dear to them, are thrown into sorrow and distress."

The first two years of the War saw the first four names on the "Honours Board" (which was given to the church by an anonymous donor), but it was the last two years that brought the terrible toll of casualties, which so devastated the parish, now numbering twenty-six in total.

However, the first reminders of the War came to our Parish on the 17th Of October, 1914, when a family of Belgian refugees from Antwerp arrived at the Vicarage. This was Mr Ghyoot, his wife and five children, 3 girls and 2 boys, with only what they stood up in. This galvanised the Parish, the usual committee was formed, donations requested and all the requirements of those good people were catered for. Offers of help came in many ways. Mrs Burton, the Vicars wife, gave them the loan of the Cedars at Darliston, free of rates and taxes, value £27.8s.0d. Mrs Sarah Sandford gave £25. Some people gave donations, others contributed so much a week (usually a shilling or six-pence), various articles of furniture and household requisites were loaned. Mrs Darlington and Mrs Hough gave a quart of milk per day.

Mrs's Allwood, Cooper and Weston gave bread weekly. Mr Lightfoot and Miss Woollam 3cwts (3 hundred weights equivalent to 152.4 kilograms), of coal a week. A bicycle was loaned plus money to keep it in repair. Dr. Bennett also donated, and kindly gave his professional services free of charge. The family were very well liked and the children went to Lower Heath School. They were not able to return to Belgium until March 1917.

But with the deteriorating nature of the "News Bulletins" from the battle front, and ever-increasing causalities, the concentrated desire was to do whatever they could. A meeting was held in Lower Heath School, where it was decided to collect a sum of money for the "Fauls Boys" who were serving their country in the War. Well over a hundred people responded (all named) and, to such a degree that it enabled the Parish of Fauls to send each soldier a ten-shilling Bank of England note

"THERE IS ALWAYS A BOOK ON THE SHELF...!"

as a Christmas present. This was repeated for the two remaining years of War.

Yes, it is good "we remember" and, we must also bear in mind that these lads were "all volunteers."

This awful War so indelibly weaved into the fabric of our local history, tragically kept our "Honours Board" activated until, "the eleventh hour, of the eleventh day, of the eleventh month in 1918". Mrs Dutton of Darliston, a widow having lost her husband in a train accident, her son Tom was the first on the "Honours Board." One day she was distressed, sobbing her heart out, leaning over her wicket gate.

A youth passing on his bicycle shouted to her, "Cheer up Mrs Dutton, the armistice has been signed." But for Mrs Dutton it was too late to save her second son Joe, in her hand was the telegram informing her of his death. Mrs Dutton's granddaughters and her neighbours conveyed this sad story to me

"Lest we forget"

CHAPTER 13

February 2009: Goffin v Taylor

On the 29th September 1875, Robert Taylor at the age of 26, was appointed Headmaster of Lower Heath School. In this capacity, he would stay until his retirement, 44 years later, in 1919. He worked under a Management Committee of which the Chairman was Thomas Hugh Sandford Esq., husband to Sarah Sandford, his second wife, and with the now in place Government directives, which had slowly been introduced over the years.

Robert Taylor had replaced Robert Goffin, who had held the position for 37 years, under the management of the Hill family of Hawkstone, of which Anne, Viscountess Hill, who had engaged him, and to whom he was answerable. At the distance of 133 years, I am tempted to make comparisons between these two excellent Headmasters, as instanced by HMIS, reports, school and school management log book and occasions when journalists put pen to paper.

So tempted am I, only because they were completely different people, products of their own characters, time, and tide. That they both achieved high prominence and much favourable correspondence in adapting to one of the most demanding jobs – in any community – in guiding our Lower Heath School through 81 years of dedicated input. Yes, the progress and fortunes of the school were in very capable hands that my admiration for them both is equal.

We knew nothing of Robert Goffin until he arrived at Lower Heath School from Great Yarmouth, in 1839. However, we knew much more about Robert Taylor, who was a local lad, born only 2 miles from Lower Heath School at Prees Wood. His father was a brick maker and carried on his business at the rear of Brickfield Cottage. His kilns, which are still there today, were adjacent to the footpath which was a shortcut through to Prees Village. I am sure I can safely assume that this footpath would have been well worn by a young Robert Taylor as he journeyed to and from Prees School, where he received his early education.

He was a most talented pupil at Prees School. First under Headmasters Samuel Rookes, and then under Mr. Hooks, where he became a monitor, teaching the younger children, and then a pupil teacher. He was also singled out for special encouragement, by Archdeacon Allen (Vicar of Prees Parish and Archdeacon of Salop), culminating in him attending Saltney Teacher Training College, Birmingham in 1871. Here he obtained his Teaching Certificate which by now was essential to qualify him for Headmastership.

Archdeacon Allen – Vicar of Prees Parish and Archdeacon of Salop.

Robert Goffin however, did not possess this, and possibly the combination of this and the death of the 2nd Viscount Hill and subsequent management change, hastened his retirement. But, testament to his capabilities, Industry Hall was referred to locally and afar, "as that magnificent Institution under Robert Goffin."

When in the evening of his teaching, his school became the subject of HMIS and he experienced four of these visits. They were all excellent and at the last one on the 12th March, 1875, Rev. R. Temple expressed, "satisfaction in the manner and response of the children" and informed the Master his, "Report would be a good one and the Grant large."

Also, during his day, the word punishment was never mentioned with the Hill family having instructed their teachers to treat the children tenderly. If, on the odd occasion extra firmness was needed, their Chaplain was despatched to the school, and a good dressing down in front of the whole school sufficed. So, all in all, Lower Heath School under Robert Goffin had achieved every requirement of the Hill family for their estate children, enabling them to procure a livelihood and fit them to be good citizens. He also applied a bit of magic in getting those children to sing so well, as does the present day Headteacher, all resulting in a happy school.

On Robert Goffin's retirement, he continued to live in his quarters at the school, often sitting in on the School Management Committee Meetings. After four years, and for the last 8 years of his life, he lived in the beautiful Victorian lodge at Weston-under-Redcastle, owned by the Hill family, and I am sure that by allowing him to live out his years in this property, they were showing the high esteem and regard in which they held him.

"THERE IS ALWAYS A BOOK ON THE SHELF...!"

Weston Gate Lodge, Gate to Hawkestone Hall

Interestingly, he was not without some private income, he owned two cottages at Prees Wood, also a half share in a threshing machine business and he probably received private tuition fees as well. He remained a bachelor and died on October 22nd, 1889.

Robert Taylor however, was a married man, having married Miss Batho of Prees Mill, eight years after becoming the headmaster in 1875. This was to the delight of the whole village of Prees with most of them assembled either in the Congregational Church or outside it. The choir was in attendance, with Miss Hinks on the harmonium, arches were erected festooned with greenery and flowers and suitable mottoes and motifs. The happy couple left on the 11.55 a.m. train from Prees, to spend their honeymoon in London.

PART TWO
Mr Robert Taylor

CHAPTER 14

March 2009: Mr Robert Taylor Early Days

Robert Taylor was appointed headmaster of the then Viscountess Hill's Church of England School, Lower Heath, in September 1875, having cut his teeth as headmaster of Clive School for the previous three years. By now the school had been placed within the government system and run by a Board of Managers. He had inherited a "good ship", passed into his charge after being a family run school for 76 years. The Hills of Hawkestone had done a good job in building and promoting it as a place of industry and learning, which had become the envy of many an Estate in the late 18th century and referred to as the "Magnificent Institution", locally and afar. It also became the hub of community life for all the various entertainments and meetings for the hamlets of Mickley, Fauls, Darliston, Sandford, Lower Heath and beyond, and this all helped defray the building's maintenance costs.

The man clearing his desk and moving out was Robert Goffin, who left behind a register with the names of 174 children, 145 of them from Lord Hill's tenantry; 19 from Squire Thomas Sandford and a few others. His curriculum, which I thought was very comprehensive for that day, consisted of reading, writing, arithmetic, history, geography, needlework, religious knowledge, English, school drill, knitting (taught to boys and girls), poetry and Robert Goffin's speciality SINGING. I did just wonder if it was Robert Goffin's way of counter-balancing those harsh, forbidding, poverty-stricken days of the Victorians.

Recently I heard a Radio 4 programme about Education when the presenter finally pulled the strings together for me when he said, "If I had anything to do with education, I would make singing the central plank" and I borrow those words, because for me that sums up Robert Goffin, he seemed to have a "pied-piper" effect on his pupils, he led, and he did not use punishment. But it worked, earning him the admiration of all. Cathy the present Headteacher, wrote recently about her recording a C.D. of the current school kids. This was brilliant and I took my little grandson several times to listen to them and he loved it! I am sure Robert Goffin would have been proud of us; indeed, he certainly would.

So, like "ships that pass in the night," Robert Taylor now sat in the headmaster's chair and began to set out his credentials. At the least it must have been a bit of a culture shock for the children as Robert was a very strict disciplinarian. Within a few days, the children knew that misbehaviour in any shape or form would not be tolerated. He demonstrated that he was prepared to use whatever type of punishment he had at his disposal, including despatching the dust from a boy's rear-end if he stepped out of line.

It was important to know which side of the fence you were on; and then all was well. But for all that, it worked and worked well, for behind that austere veneer, Robert Taylor was a kindly man. He willingly made himself available for advice and help, not only to the children and parents, but the community in general; he took their welfare to his heart.

Just to mention, one very important area where he endeared himself was by forming the "Lower Heath Cow Club (LHCC)" for the many small holders and, often a cottager who would have a single cow. The loss of a cow would have caused considerable distress in those days, but now for a few pence

"THERE IS ALWAYS A BOOK ON THE SHELF...!"

and LHCC carved into the horn of the beast, upon its death, the money was there for its replacement.

In other words, Robert Tayler set his stall out and became much, much more than a headmaster – he became a pillar of the community. He was also a good churchman, and played the organ for many years. He never had a pony and trap, preferring to walk everywhere; never accepting a lift. He walked up to a few days before his death in 1939 at the age of 89 and so, I intend to do a lot of walking!

CHAPTER 15
April 2009: School Management

The whole process of changing the school management at Lower Heath Church of England School slipped into place seemingly very smoothly. Robert Taylor, the new headmaster, was always destined to be a "bit special," with a C.V. fitting him for any eventuality, and he seems to have "hit the deck running." Mind you, he had got to brief a formidable array of managers to whom he had to make a quarterly report.

These were led by Thomas H. Sandford, Esq., with Archdeacon Allen of Prees, Rev. J. B. Lennard, Vicar of Fauls, Viscount Hill, J.P.H. Lonsdale Esq., with ten others on the team – usually the tenantry of the big farms in the Parish were on the list. And so, on a rotating basis, about one third of the above names would attend. But, of course, the most important were the visitations of HMIS, who monitored the progress of the classes and allocated grants accordingly. These grants had got to be matched by public contributions and parents had to contribute a few pence. So, all in all, the financing of the school was delicately balanced with a mishmash of arrangements, but it all worked very well, to the benefit of all the children in Fauls Parish.

I loved Robert Taylors first report, which I have in front of me, which he used to address his first managers meeting.

"Chairman and Gentlemen, I ought to mention that I have, during the past three months, acted in every way in accordance with the agreement made with me by Archdeacon Allen and

"THERE IS ALWAYS A BOOK ON THE SHELF...!"

Rev. J.B. Lennard. This agreement in short that I was subject to approval of your body, find everything necessary for the complete and thorough working of the school in accordance with the Education Department, pay all expenses and receive all subscriptions, children's pence, and government grants. All expenses are set down and itemised for the whole of the present quarter, ending December 31st 1875".

He also goes on to state, besides himself there are four other teachers regularly employed by the school an assistant mistress, taking charge of infants, and sewing, and three other paid monitors namely Elizabeth Moreton, Lazia Bennett and George Oakley. They were from Sand Lane, Prees Green and Fauls Green respectively.

Of those 174 names on the School Register, the average attendance has at present been 145, with boys 69, girls 31 and infants 45. The total amount of school pence received during the quarter is £19 5s 3d. Of this sum £8 14s 9d has been paid by the boys, £5 7s 9d. by the girls and £5 2s 9d by the infants.

That was the business of how the school was run and, going to be run. But it did not happen without a lot of hard work by a few people; namely T.H. Sandford, Esq., with Archdeacon Allen of Prees, Rev. J. B. Lennard, Vicar of Fauls and Robert Taylor the headmaster, who pulled all the strings together. Well, the "whole Parish" had now got to develop a culture not only of giving, but of "giving regularly." The vacuum left by the Hill family had got to be filled by voluntary subscription, otherwise the threat was that the Government would put their own Board of Managers in, which would cost much more than they currently paid their current board.

Likewise, the few pence the children were expected to pay was a difficult one. They were mostly the children of agriculture, timber, mill, and forestry workers who toiled long hours for a pittance of pay. But a delicate balance had to be struck, if a child did not bring his or her pence for the quarter, Robert Taylor was authorised to send them home. Luckily, it was only the few, and often the family money problems would be due to drink, with the Vicar often writing about this problem.

Robert Taylor would take it upon himself to educate these parents that the dubious benefits of the extra alcoholic beverage, at the expense of their children, was not a good idea. Nobody, but nobody, argued with Robert Taylor; and finally, they paid up.

The now Dowager Viscountess Hill (Anne) must have envisaged monetary problems for the school. As she had defrayed every expense on her departure and made £50 available annually, paid in four instalments, to help underpin the progress of the school and its new management.

In other words, "the welfare of the school and its children had forever been in her thoughts."

CHAPTER 16

May 2009: Raising Funds

To write about Robert Taylor, who was headmaster of Lower Heath School for 44 years, is not only a pleasure for me, but it is comparatively easy. He is well within the grasp of time, that allows me to meander closely in his footsteps, look over his shoulder, and monitor those years he devoted to the school, from 30th September, 1875 to 31st July 1919.

Although I was only seven when he died at 89, there were still lots of people about who had been taught by him, including the man I "went to the tools" with, George Ward. **

For them, to reminisce about Robert Taylor, was almost second nature. Plus, the legacy of the school log books, which affords me a non-stop mine of information. His hand having made on average, 80 to 90 entries every month, which recorded the history of the school day by day, and the character of the man so very much in charge, that rippled throughout the community.

Robert Taylors first year as headmaster was, as it was always going to be, a big success in all ways. His first visitation by HMIS by Mr Colville and Mr Booth, was very complementary, saying: "This school is in a thoroughly efficient condition as to instruction and discipline," his Management Committee on the 30th September 1876 voted unanimously to give him a gratuity of £20. But he must understand that it is not a precedent for any sum that may or may not be paid in the future. All to which Mr Taylor expressed his heart-felt thanks.

It happened again in 1878, and an annual figure of £10 gratuity was to be added each year to his salary of £110. So, wheels turning nicely, the teaching taken care of, now it had got to be paid for; enter Archdeacon Allen.

First, he circulated the occupiers of properties, not only with a written suggestion as to how much they should give, in keeping with their ability, and secondly, he presented himself on their doorstep to collect it! Their names were listed and entered in the manager's book and, in all, there were 24 subscribers that resulted in £34 4s 6d. paid to the treasurer on December 18th 1875.

The above sum of money, plus Viscountess Hills annual £50 donation, school pence of £77 plus a box for donations at the school and the Government grant – value not known – represented the income. The expenditure, mostly wages, stationary, cleaning, insurance, fuel, lighting plus the fitting of a window in Industry Hall, and a new installation of a urinal. Collectively this resulted in a nice healthy bank balance in favour of the school at the National Provincial Bank of England at Whitchurch. These accounts continued in a similar way for the next 28 years.

As time progressed, Robert Taylor was promoted to a first-class teacher. The four quarterly management teams meetings with the master's report were reduced to one annually, unless something exceptional arose. Robert was firmly in control, teaching, managing, equal to any eventuality and most importantly, which he appreciated most of all, he had the complete backing of all the parents. In fact, it was said that if Robert Taylor punished a child, when they got home, they received a similar dose of medicine from their parents. In fact, one mother requested Mr Taylor to punish her son John. He caned him and, there is no evidence that he ever returned for another dose!

"THERE IS ALWAYS A BOOK ON THE SHELF...!"

Staying with punishment, in Robert Taylors first year as headmaster, he took his cane to five boys, with the appropriate number of strokes, depending on the misdemeanour. In his second year, with only seven days of that year remaining, he did mention punishing a boy for continued negligence of home lessons.

So, knowledge that the availability of the cane was there, acted as a deterrent. But the cane was the most extreme of various punishments. My favourite was that a pupil would have to stay in after school and write down the name of every estuary around the British Isles. I think I would have enjoyed that!

** **Editor's Note** I love the intrinsic links and circles that form over time in the countryside. Part of Geoge Wards work was as a wheelwright and he worked in partnership with the blacksmith Mr Williams based at the Smithy at Weston-under-Redcastle to complete each wheel. Dad knew Mr. Williams all his life and as a young lad he used to go down to the Smithy at Prees Green with Tommy Speed, where they were "roped into" working the bellows to keep the fire coals bright. Mr Williams would reward Tommy and dad with a "proper blacksmith made nail," which was treasured as it was perfect for boring holes through conkers; an essential tool to facilitate autumn games. Little did dad know at the time, that he would go on to marry Mr Williams' daughter Mary and become best mates with his youngest son Peter.

Mr Williams at Prees Green Smithy looking to camera

CHAPTER 17

June 2009: Sir Francis Sandford

As parents, we are all usually desirous that our children do well, at least better than we did, and achieve their own individual potential. Hopefully teaching will unlock and encourage this potential, which is an art beyond price. That Robert Taylor and his sister Mary Anne his assistant achieved this to a considerable degree, is beyond doubt, and this is evidenced by the many positive HMIS' reports.

So, I am sure their parents John and Victoria Taylor, who lived long enough to be aware of the success they both achieved, would have been thrilled to bits with them. And, as such, there was no need for them to get involved in their father's business; the back-breaking work of moulding clay into bricks.

I note with interest two entries of Robert Taylors in the school log book, first in December 8th 1884 (nine years after becoming headmaster): "Master received first parchment certificate – raised to First Class." The second on April 9th 1885: "Sir Francis Richard Sandford, Lady Margaret Sandford, Mrs Sarah Sandford, and Rev. H. Burton – now Vicar of Fauls, having replaced Rev. Lennard – visited the school this morning. Half day – holiday given" – no elaboration whatsoever.

Well! Sir Francis Sandford was later to be elevated to the Peerage (1st Baron Sandford 1891 to 1893; upon his death the Barony expired) for his services to Education and the successful implementation of the Elementary Education Act of 1870. He had been given the task, by the then Liberal

Government, whilst he was Permanent Under-Secretary of State for the Committee of Council on Education. In other words, he was the top man of that day and obviously aware, through his inspectors' reports, of Robert Taylors ability. Hence, he just dropped in for a morning at Lower Heath School to see for himself. He must have been well satisfied, in dismissing the school for a half days holiday. I have enjoyed elaborating for him!

Sandford Hall Front Elevation

How Robert Tayler and his staff achieved this success was amazing, taking into consideration the very high rate of absenteeism for many different reasons. Also, the HMIS exercised their now increased powers. The annual fixed day for inspection was eventually replaced by two unannounced visits. Then, seemingly forever, people were just dropping in; all well-meaning, but it must have added some distraction to the working of the school. Yes, it was welcome to the early pressures on the educator and educated so relevant and forever with us, and, although manifested in different ways today, the name of the game was the same.

The now all-important schooling system bringing opportunity to all children, was nicely and legally in position, but it also

"THERE IS ALWAYS A BOOK ON THE SHELF...!"

had to blend in with the ordered pattern and structure of the times. The annual seasons came and went, having various impacts on the school and the corresponding absenteeism diligently recorded by Robert Taylors' hand.

Winter always took a heavy toll with weather and sickness problems, with many entries such as, "very cold, rain – small attendance;" "often snow – school closed;" as many as sixty or more children were absent with colds, influenzas, whooping cough, measles or worst of all scarlet fever and diphtheria, which again closed the school.

Also, the winter sports of gentlemen, gave entries quite often such as: "Lord Hill requested, any number of boys up to thirty for driving game," and in warmer times, "May 6th – upper class absent planting potatoes", "July, boys sent to work in the Hawkestone gardens for Lord Hill, "many absent in the hay fields (all of the top class), very poor school attendance throughout the month." On the 8th December, 1885 Robert Taylor made a further entry into the school log book, "14 boys sent to drive the game at Soulton."

Hawkestone Hall Arial View Showing Extent of Gardens

August holidays accounted for much of the corn harvest but come September and October, many children were absent gathering potatoes and gleaning, another entry, "absent gleaning." The occupation of gleaning was to salvage the ears of corn shed during harvest, so that none may be lost.

Other entries were, "many children absent coppicing" this meant the gathering of firewood to lay store against the cold of winter, also fruit picking, especially damsons. "Goodness" as my mother used to say "Children don't know they are born today." Anyway, I am now going absent to plant my onion sets.

CHAPTER 18
July/August 2009: A Family Job

It would be difficult to imagine a family more involved with a little country school than the Taylor family at Lower Heath. Robert Taylor would be succeeded by his son, also Robert – he became known as Bert – having been headmasters for a collective 75 years! But in the early years during the latter part of the 19th century, the Taylors influence appeared to be total. When Robert Taylor became headteacher, his sister Mary Anne became his assistant and their younger brother John became a monitor (sadly, he died young at 16).

In the early 1880's both Robert and Mary Anne married and proceeded to produce off-spring, nine in total over a period of eleven years. All these children were entered on the school admission register before they were three years old. They all, in their turn, became monitors, progressing to pupil teacher at the school, travelling to Shrewsbury and Whitchurch for exams before going to college and gaining qualification. At least four of their children eventually became head teachers.

In addition to the family offspring, thirty of his pupils became qualified teachers during his 44 years as headteacher. Yes, his teaching skills were absorbed by many other pupils who went on to earn fame for themselves including, Tom Oakley, who became a member of parliament. Hence, as the old local folk used to say, "you could tell a scholar who had enjoyed the influence of Robert Taylor."

Robert Taylor and his wife Eliza Jane had three children, Eleanor, Eliza, and Robert (Bert) and they lived in the school house at Lower Heath.

Mary Anne married William Steventon, whose family were small holders and ran a thrashing machine business. They lived at Woodside Cottage, down the lane adjacent to the school, where they had six children, Harold, Ellis, Millicent, Wilfred, Eleanor, and Winifred. On the birth of her first child on the 20th March 1884, into the pram he went, and off to school through a special gate she had at the bottom of the playground; no nannies in that day! In the end it was one in the pram, one on the pram and four trotting by her side. I love this story, told to me by Mrs Davies (nee Annie Active) who also taught at Lower Heath school for 40 years.

Mrs Steventon was the Infants teacher and looked over the girls' sewing lessons. She, like her brother, was very strict, and played it "by the book." If an odd parent should create any "ado," the family ranks closed shut – end of story. During Mrs Steventons brief absences producing children, the millers' daughter – Robert's wife Eliza Jane, would step in as cover, which she was very capable of doing. But, by and large, Robert Taylor and his sister were blessed with good health, and Robert hardly missed a day in his 44 years.

Robert Taylors well chronicled success as a headmaster was based on his scholarship and those well tested Victorian virtues of hard work and discipline, from which he never deviated. This enabled him to take the school forward onto another plain, not forgetting the wonderful foundation he inherited, created by the Hill family of Hawkestone, notably Lady Anne Hill and her school master Robert Goffin.

"THERE IS ALWAYS A BOOK ON THE SHELF...!"

Of course, everything evolves from within the four walls of a classroom with children congregated together from all parts of the scattered Parish of Fauls, conveyed by their only means of transport, sometimes as far as two miles away, their legs!!

But each one knew, if they worked hard and did well, the appropriate praise would be forthcoming. Indeed, countless times Robert Taylor wrote, "class has done well." If, on the other hand, the odd individual did misbehave, the master had his different forms of punishment to persuade them it was not a good idea. The good idea, was to take on board as much education as each could individually cope with; then all was well.

CHAPTER 19

September 2009: Homework

One of the first things Lower Heath School children became aware of under their new headmaster, was that school was not just from 9.00am to 3.30pm, it was on-going. When they went home in the afternoon, their butty bag was loaded with what the master referred to as "home lessons" and to neglect them; well, punishment was available. However, it was a big success, enabling Robert to write: "It is most rewarding when children have got the grasp of a subject prior to teaching it."

Not all subjects were suitable for home lessons, but he also prescribed a large amount of spelling and dictation for home. At holiday time they would be loaded up with poetry to learn, with the expectation it would be repeated accurately on reassembling.

There is every indication that Robert Taylor's methods, embroidered with his own particular magic, were a huge success. But, as with everything, it is a two-way thing. I just loved it when in the 1880's, in the beautiful month of May, the children came to school laden with flowers, in the days when the countryside was awash with wild flowers, their purpose to decorate the school to celebrate the anniversaries of their teachers' marriages. If that was not a little bit of magic, I am at a loss to know what is.

In 1882 Robert Taylor made another valuable contribution to arrest more of the children's out of school attention by his introduction of the school library. So, with the children's thoughts well concentrated, both in school and at home, and of course the most important ingredient the teachers, the ground was well prepared for the next annual visitation from HMIS.

These reports from the Education department were delivered to the management of the school, where they were read out either by Mrs Sarah Sandford or the Vicar. They would then congratulate the children and the teachers on these very favourable accounts, at the same time remarking that such reports, "Should prove a powerful stimulus to continued exertions;" of course, they never missed the punchline, also it was for the honour and the wellbeing of the school. So having taken their bow, the children, and teachers, who were also examined, their inference was that the hard work must continue. It must have been a long, hard day for all concerned.

The following extracts are given as an example of the comments and are dated December 8th 1885. Mixed School – "An excellent school, thoroughly and intelligently taught in every subject," Infant Class – "The infants are, as usual, thoroughly well taught and, in excellent order."

CHAPTER 20
October 2009: Discipline

To say Robert Taylor gave and demanded total commitment from his staff and pupils would be a gross understatement, as his many log book entries bear out. There was no hiding place, no escape; in fact, he even concentrates my thoughts, well over a hundred years into the future! I am quite pleased about that.

His Victorian pupils which encompassed the last quarter of the 19th century and Robert Taylor's first 25 years as headmaster, were made very, very aware of this. Even the demands on the children's time, through the season's requirements on the land, were somewhat partially catered for by home lessons. In other words, no matter what the days agenda was, albeit planting or harvesting potatoes, gleaning the fields for shed corn, fruit picking, especially damsons, driving game or even illness, they must dovetail some time in for school work.

With the package also came lots of encouragement and appeals to the children's initiative, but if this was not reciprocal, there were corrective measures in place to help them, punishment which came in different and novel ways, was available for all those who misbehaved.

Yes discipline! This became more essential under Robert Taylor because he had inherited a school of children who were leaving at 10-11 years of age, and this would soon rise to 13-14, under new guidelines, increasing the workload and only offset by one extra teacher. Whilst under Lady Anne Hill

"THERE IS ALWAYS A BOOK ON THE SHELF...!"

and schoolmaster Robert Goffin, the children were encouraged to do their best in an easy-going atmosphere, now with the state system in place, they were not only encouraged but their best was demanded of them.

Any disruption to this aim was immediately jumped on and the Log Book entries record forever the names of boys who were foolish enough to step out of line, and the punishment they received. This came in the form of a cane, anything from 2-6 strokes applied to various parts of their bodies for extreme offences. For other misdeeds, recreation would be withdrawn, stopping in at playtime or after school, no football, no one to speak to you for a given length of time, and/or holding up a board in class for several minutes.

But in all fairness to the Master and pupils, it was mostly a deterrent; few were prepared to run the gauntlet and in addition the Vicar scrutinized every entry, and commented on the pupil in front of the class. Thus, the extremes of fighting, bad language, throwing stones and defiance of authority, were kept to a minimum whether it was in school, or out of school as the Police Constable would call in to mention reports of bad behaviour by children journeying to and from school as well.

On balance it would appear the most important aspect of this unfolding tapestry of a Victorian school "discipline," administered by Robert Taylor, seemingly was a work of art. Firstly his very "being" and "air of authority," sufficed to instil this very necessary ingredient discipline, in most of the children. Then defining the line between misbehaviour and high spirits usually accounted for a caution, a warning or severe warning before corporal punishment was administered.

Even after all that he once wrote in his Log Book: "I am trying to give up corporal punishment."

But eventually the few forced his hand, these few being regular offenders and it seemed to run in particular families where several sets of brothers were concerned. So, it is nice to write that, despite the discipline, some of those disciplined did go on to get Awards for good work in the classroom. In summary Robert Taylor never gave up on a pupil, with first the encouragement and then the demand.

Even Tom Oakley, the Lower Heath scholar who went on to be a Member of Parliament, had the dust knocked out of his pants several times by Robert Taylor and, as my mother said, "there is always a silver lining for those who are prepared to work and discipline themselves."

Anyhow, I doubt whether there was a better character-building machine for youngsters than the Taylor regime, in the father and son reign of 75 years at Lower Heath School.

CHAPTER 21

December 2009/January 2010: Raising Funds for The Infants New Classroom

As Lower Heath School progressed through the last years of the 19th and turn of the 20th century, it brought the usual mixture of highs and lows. During this time, the school and parish had mourned the loss of two of the schools most important benefactors, in Sir Francis Sandford and Lady Anne Hill. In fact, for many years after, it was still referred to as Lady Hill's School, in respect of her forty years devotion to the education of local children.

But, in 1894, there developed a problem, which grew in momentum, concentrating the managers thinking. For several years they had discussed the reports from the Education Department, in respect of the school buildings.

With Lower Heath being a Church of England School, these HMIS Reports went to the Vicar of Fauls, Rev. Harold Burton, now Chairman of the managers, and whilst he took great pleasure in conveying the excellent content to the teaching staff and children, I doubt whether he enjoyed the "tail bits" of these reports; because, having examined the teachers and staff, they then turned their attention to the school premises and equipment. Frequently this was not good reading for the Vicar to take with his breakfast, nor his managers. The Inspectors wrote: "I trust the Managers may shortly be in a position to make the buildings as generally satisfactory as the teaching is," – shortly was to eventually span twenty years.

"Any proposals which the managers have to improve the school premises should be submitted to the Department for approval, the managers are once again reminded of the insufficiency and unsuitability of equipment and are requested to give this their early consideration" ... this tone continued with the Inspectors condemning the Infants old Industry Hall for teaching purposes. Of course, this came with the threat of a Government Board being put in to run the school, if a new infant's class was not built.

The Vicar did not like this and so he read the "riot act" to the managers and the Parish, as he knew a Government Board would cost parishioners a lot more.

In a nut shell, these reports now condemned the old Industry Hall, which was used for teaching the infants. The ceilings were too low, and had no ventilation. The cost of a new classroom had got to be found – Oh dear!

So, the firefighting had begun. A meeting of the rate payers was called for Monday 3rd May, 1898 at the school, to consider the method of raising funds for the erection of a new infant's school, to fulfil the requirements of the Education Department, with the chair occupied by the Rev. Harold Burton.

Also invited – in an advisory capacity – was Mr. Hall the Hawkstone Estate Agent, who urged the necessity of the work being done voluntarily, if the expense of a School Board was to be avoided. Money was not available from the Hill family now. However, he agreed that a voluntary rate be levied in the school district to be paid in two instalments, the first after the harvest of 1897, the second at the discretion of the building committee at an interval of not less than six months, but so that the total raised does not exceed £120.

"THERE IS ALWAYS A BOOK ON THE SHELF...!"

This all came with an appeal to owners of property to pay two thirds of the rate levied on their tenants towards the new build. It was also stated that costs would be considerably reduced if the conveyance of materials could be done free of cost. The response was brilliant, with every bit of voluntary labour possible used, including the haulage of bricks. Miss Thomas, of whom you will hear more of, wrote, "It took eleven thousand, four hundred bricks" and her uncle was paid seven shillings and sixpence to unload them. These bricks, when nicely in position, would become an up-to-date, modern Infants classroom, every penny of costs defrayed by the people of Fauls Parish. In total fourteen people promised assistance, and of these Mr. Hall prepared the plans for the new classroom and invited three builders to tender and supervised the work.

Mr. R. Powell of Prees submitted the successful estimate of £145, against £147 Tommy Bros. of Wem and £171 Mr. Dodd of Whitchurch and on the 26th July 1897, Mr. Powell was invited to attend the office at Weston-under-Redcastle to receive instructions from Mr. Hall and sign the contract.

At last! the job was up and running.

All the delicate business of persuading, cajoling people to agree to part with their money seemed to be in the very capable hands of the Rev. Harold Burton, whose wife had already started the fund, by donating the proceeds from three previous annual concerts given by her church choir, held in the school.

But Robert Taylor, the school master, was charged with the business of knocking on doors to collect this money, for which he was paid £5.

One can detect much concern to do with the whole project, so much so, that I approached a local quantity surveyor as to what the cost would be in today's parlance. Without hesitation he said, "more than £50,000", that provides the context, hence I now have a full understanding of their concern. Log book references tell me that, "the noise of busy workmen did affect lessons" and the school had an extended summer holiday of one week.

The builder, Mr Powell of Prees, had done an excellent job. He had stitched the new extension onto the original Industry Hall, build by Richard Hill in 1799, and abutted to Lady Hills big classroom extension of 1840.

Lower Heath School, New Infants Classroom at Rear (with tall chimney)

So, Inspectors, managers and parishioners had done a wonderful job to fulfil the requirements of that day, and on the 10th January, 1898, Robert Taylor wrote: "Infants began work in the new classroom". Miss Thomas was one of those Infants, having been admitted to the school on the 9th May 1898.

"THERE IS ALWAYS A BOOK ON THE SHELF...!"

Just to mention the last entry of the Inspectors Report prior to the completion of the new Infants classroom was: "The class does satisfactory, in spite of the defective accommodation. Better premises are in course of erection." These inspectors continued to be very critical with other aspects of the school, but these were light by comparison, at the end of the twenty years span mentioned. But on January 10th 1898, the infants began working in the new classroom.

So, Industry Hall just missed its centenary as a classroom, but it is still a very integral part of the school after well over 200 years. It was unanimously resolved that a stone be placed in the gable end of the new Infants School, having the following inscription:

"Industry Hall"
This School was founded in the year 1799
by Sir Richard Hill, Bart.
And was maintained entirely by the Hill Family,
until the year 1875.
The Infant Room was erected
by voluntary subscription AD.1897.

Robert Taylor, who had now completed his first twenty-five years as Headmaster, wrote at the beginning of the summer holidays in 1899: "Examined classes this week, result very gratifying." He also wrote: "Mrs. Sarah Sandford kindly gave the scholars and mothers – as she usually did – a tea party." But this was to be a bit special, as she wished to commemorate the 80th birthday of Queen Victoria and the centenary of the school, which had opened on the 6th November, 1799.

CHAPTER 22

February 2010: Deed Of Gift from The Hill Family

The staff and management of Lower Heath School, indeed the whole Parish of Fauls, were rightly proud of their new infant classroom; regardless of the financial burden imposed upon them. But, after all their endeavours and anxieties of being equal to all eventualities experienced by a voluntary run school, these were to disappear overnight. With the event of the Education Act of 1902 (Balfour Act), the government took over all expenses of the school. So, the management which had been in place since 1875, would now relinquish their duties.

At their last meeting on January 3rd 1903, and after submitting his last construction report Robert Taylor concluded by thanking the managers for their hearty, unceasing co-operation, and support for the past 28 years. Oh! And the last comments from the chairman, were to report that the school premises had been transferred, as a Deed of Gift, from the Hawkestone Estate to seven trustees.

The trust deed had been executed and was read and considered. According to its provisions, the following became the four active managers Rev. H. Burton, Mrs. Sarah Sandford, Captain Heywood-Lonsdale and Mr. Higginson, a tenant of Mrs. Sandford. To complete the plaudits all round, the Chairman, Rev. H. Burton, made favourable remarks about Robert

"THERE IS ALWAYS A BOOK ON THE SHELF...!"

Taylor, "as to the complete satisfaction as to the way in which he had carried out his duties as headmaster."

Just to mention, in all those 28 years, Robert Taylor had only applied for an increase in salary once, this was to the amount of the contributions required by the Teacher's Superannuation Act of £3.00 per annum. He must have been pleasantly surprised when the committee awarded his salary a raise of three pounds per quarter. They also expressed their pleasure that a pension fund had been provided by H.M. Government and in taking over the expenses of the school.

In fact, Robert Taylor had never put a foot wrong, his influence on the school and children, also their parents, was immense. He was forever concerned with their welfare, a knock on his door meant help with whatever powers he had to bestow, usually in the form of guidance or advice.

The most important thing that concentrated the whole locality, was the demise in the fortunes of Hawkstone Estates, during the last years of the 19th and beginning of the 20th centuries. The Hill family had been wonderful, caring landlords. It was unbelievable that, after three and a half centuries, their vast Estates, with a series of sales from 1890-1906, were now finished.

The tenantry had travelled through unknown territory, but fortunately many of them had been able to become owner/occupiers, hence the worries of whether they had got a roof over their heads was resolved in most cases. Because the Hill family had a policy of encouraging cottagers to become smallholders – praised by agricultural historians – so much so, I could pass 39 of these within a few minutes from home, on my bike, and there were scores more across the former estate.

The Hill's approach had created close knit communities, and the smallholders with their few acres, usually in little fields, hedged with damson trees at regular intervals, as a good crop of damsons would pay the rent for a year. With their few cows, pigs, poultry and always a good garden with vegetables and fruit, this kept the smallholders well fed.

When stock needed to go to auction, they would join together with the droving, to either Wem, Whitchurch or Market Drayton. A few of them had a pony and trap, and they would take the weaners and store pigs. Of course, their lot was a dawn to dusk activity, as they also worked part time on the bigger farms or wherever a job needed doing. Also, if a holder was having trouble with a calving, farrowing or any other illness of stock, he knew his neighbours would be there to help, even sitting up with stock all night if necessary.

And sadly, if a cow died, the Robert Taylor's Cow Club, which observers described as the best in the land, provided the money to replace it.

CHAPTER 23

March 2010: A Closed Shop

The early 20th century and its progression brought considerable change to our little Parish of Fauls and its average population of 500 plus. The most important, being predominantly agriculturally based, with the bigger farmers and smallholders now became owner-occupiers, albeit this usually meant instead of paying rent to the Hill family of Hawkstone, this now became interest on borrowed money. This new atmosphere created a bit more urgency, gave people a bit more self-respect and the will to get on. Also, the ingredient of having Edward VII on the throne from 1901 tended to add a more colourful dimension.

It also seemed to benefit Lower Heath School, parents were less inclined to keep their children at home, other than for absolute necessary farm work and of course more farm machinery was now being introduced. They had also come to terms with letting their children stay at school until they were 14 years of age and of course longer if the opportunity was available.

Robert Taylor, who had forever encouraged his children to fulfil their potential, had never taken kindly to the odd parents who took their children away from school early, although he sympathised with their reasoning. Now, he had help from the Shropshire Education Department, who started to supply beautiful, scrolled certificates for children with good attendance and conduct and, there were also medals and clasps on offer.

Elementary Education Certificate Alice Jones 1907

This enabled the headmaster to record the names of seventeen children, with maximum or near minimum attendance and their awards, so there were plenty of takers. It also gave the Rev. Harold Burton and Mrs. Sarah Sandford, who officiated at these prize giving assemblies, an opportunity which they never missed, to emphasise the importance of acquiring in early life, the habits of punctuality and regularity. Also expressing pleasure at having so many recipients and the absence of bad conduct marks.

Harry Brown with maximum attendance, had won a scholarship to Wem Grammar School, he also survived the Battle of the Somme and spent his working life as a journalist. Mark Whitfield, also with full attendance was a volunteer at seventeen and I loved to hear him reminisce about being taught by Robert Taylor, he would say: "When Robert Taylor had finished with you, you didn't need a Grammar School," perhaps not quite, but people did echo these sentiments.

The well-worn track was to become first a monitor, then a pupil teacher and at about eighteen, after sitting their entrance examinations, admitted to a Teacher's Training College at Derby or Birmingham for twelve months and finally qualification.

So, I ponder, it must have been with the utmost pleasure to Robert, the headmaster, and his sister Mary, assistant mistress, when seven of their children between them, were numbers in those thirty qualified teachers. More so, as they had supplied the complete teaching staff at the school, their children in procession, occupying three pupil teacher positions in the early years of the 20th century.

Yes, it appeared to be a closed-shop at this time, from a teaching point of view. One schools inspector's observations were: "The teacher's responsibilities are great, in a school staffed by young assistants, continues to conduct the work in a very satisfactory manner, and the instruction gives evidence of much care and very fair intelligence." Another one, whilst echoing these sentiments, did mention that a "third qualified teacher was desirable for the number of children involved."

Well, education was their business, they more or less lived over the shop, and talked shop. Many times, Robert Taylor made entries into the Log Book, almost like a family diary, the names of his children, nephews, nieces: "P.T. absent today, taking examination" in whatever subject at Shrewsbury, Oswestry, Whitchurch and later their results – always passed, often with distinction – no mention of them going to a Grammar School.

CHAPTER 24

April 2010: Birds Nest

I have found it a considerable pleasure, to have meandered in the footsteps of the Taylor family, so totally involved in the running of the little country school of Lower Heath and so well documented by Robert Taylor's hand. It not only creates a wonderful tapestry of the school's workings, but also details parts of many families' early history, of which people have travelled from far and wide, in pursuit of information to fulfil their desire to explore their family tree; most of whom I am still in contact with today with cards and letters exchanged at Christmas. With the above in mind, and as I pen my observations, of by now well over a hundred years ago, I do so with an air of sadness.

So now I am attracted to one of the last of Robert Taylor's entries in the School Log Book in 1907, regarding his family. His nephew Robert W. Steventon and his son Robert Taylor. A certificate list showed that of the five subjects, Robert Steventon passed with five distinctions and Robert Taylor with two distinctions. They had both gained admission to Saltley Training College and went on to serve their country in the 1914-1918 War, in the Royal Welsh Fusiliers and the Flying Corps accordingly.

Robert Steventon eventually became Director of Education for Warwickshire, and Robert Taylor (always known as Bert), after teaching posts in Welshpool and Market Drayton, followed his father in becoming headmaster of Lower Heath School.

Of course, I got to know Bert very well indeed as he was to become my headmaster, and as such he had my utmost respect. Well, I was a creep, for years even after I had left school, I used to fetch his Sunday morning paper from Prees on my bike and my reward was always a cream bun! He always wanted to know where my two older brothers were; Harry away in the Royal Navy and Johnnie on the North-West Frontier (India), Palestine and on the Continent.

I also got to know Miss Thomas very well (Florrie), she and her family had lived adjacent to Lower Heath School back into the 18th century. She was admitted to school on the 9th July 1898 at the age of two years and ten months and remained there as a pupil of Robert Taylor until she was fourteen (1912). She had received education elsewhere, providing her with a razor-sharp brain and a memory to match. She worked as Secretary to WH Smith at Whitchurch and Florrie was a Red Cross nurse at Prees Heath during WW1.

She had experienced a colourful career which few people knew about, of which I have written elsewhere. But, as a little grey haired, elderly lady, she was persuaded and encouraged by the then headmistress, Mrs. Blower, to reminisce and talk to the children about her school days. For this, she came well prepared and I have got her notes in front of me, given to me by her family, from which I will cherry pick starting in 1900.

"We used to sit in galleries, after filing into school to the music of 'The Grand Old Duke of York.' Then we sang 'Now the Day is Over' followed by the Lord's prayer. Slates and slate pencils were handed round, on which we tried to draw objects, such as flowers and animals, we also learned to write the alphabet and figures. After, we had exercise books with lines, far apart at first, with the width gradually decreasing as we progressed. Before we left the infants, we were allowed to use pens and ink to write small sentences, such as 'June is the month of roses,' or 'A stitch in time saves nine.' By this time, we could read a little and spell small words. One boy spelt 'orange' with an 'h' and we all laughed and got into trouble."

After moving to Standard one, we had an observation notebook in which we had to write a small note on something we had seen when going to school – first celandine or a bird's nest, or as Robert Taylor put it: "The practice of allowing scholars to note each morning anything worth remark, seen by the scholars in question, is distinctly useful."

School Group

CHAPTER 25

May 2010: Headmaster Notes v Student Memories

I find it fascinating comparing Miss Thomas' notes of her school days, during the early part of the 20th century and the headmasters, Mr. Robert Taylor's, recordings in the School Log Book as it adds another interesting dimension, not only for what they wrote, but also for what they each chose not to mention.

The master would write, "Children busily working and modelling in sand."

Miss Thomas wrote: "When we began history and geography lessons, it involved lots of sand writing. We had a large tin of sand, with a jug of water and with our fingers we had to draw a map of the British Isles showing all the river estuaries, peninsulas, bays, and lakes." They also did other countries of the Empire, and Miss Thomas was highly commended for doing Australia.

In the top classes, Mr. Taylor was very keen on mental arithmetic. He would move very quickly from one child to another with additions and subtractions, and likewise with spelling. On two afternoons the classes were divided into boys for drawing and girls for sewing and knitting.

There were nearly fifty girls in the class. Florrie writes, "we used to knit woollen socks and sew aprons." The aprons were

"THERE IS ALWAYS A BOOK ON THE SHELF...!"

made from white Holland (cloth) and were sold to buy more material, but as there were inkwells in the desks and the aprons were frequently stained, then there was trouble, as they had to be sold for a lower price. This material was hard to sew and often needles were broken. It was also difficult to learn the skills of darning a large hole in a sock but two of these girls won first and second prizes at a Needlework Exhibition in Market Drayton, receiving fifteen and ten shillings respectively.

In the early part of the 20th century, the master starts to mention another lesson for the older boys in the last hour of the week; gardening. It appears Robert Taylor had purchased the little field across the road and adjacent to the Tumps. This had previously been the garden for the Toll Keeper's Cottage. Miss Thomas writes: "On the 29th of May, Oak Ball Day, we had half a day off from lessons. In the morning, if we were not wearing an oak apple, we were nettled by other children. During the afternoon, we went across to Mr. Taylor's field, where each year he grew a crop of rye. This we had to trample to flatten it and we had a lot of fun in doing it."

This saved him having to pay someone to roll it! Of course, this was then dug in to improve the fertility of the ground. Miss Thomas also wrote: "The school offices, (lavatories) were emptied once a year at Christmas. The boys wheeled barrows of sand, which had been dug up from the bottom of the playing field and formed into a circle about ten feet across. Then a man came, who had to go down a large hole underneath the lavatories and deposit the contents in the ring of sand. This was allowed to dry, then all mixed up and wheeled to the headmaster's garden." Hence the bottom corner of the playing field is several feet lower, (and still is today). Interestingly, Robert Taylor did not mention any of the above.

Anyway, teaching gardening to the older boys, usually about a dozen, was a big success. All the necessary tools had been taken delivery of, but whilst the School Inspectors could never fault Robert Taylor in the classroom, they certainly had plenty of advice for him where gardening was concerned: "The plots should be enlarged so as to allow about two rods for each dual plot, also it would be advisable to reconstruct the plots, so that their length may be at right angles to the wire fence; paths need straightening and cleaning." However, soon they were writing: "The boys are alert and observant, talk freely and seriously about their work and observations in the garden."

Some useful records were being kept regarding costs of seeds and the land occupied by different crops. A titled gentleman, from the Board of Agriculture visited, heard lessons, and addressed the children. Soon prizes were being donated and competed for, and gardening was firmly in the curriculum at Lower Heath School.

In my day, and in years to come, the Toll Keeper's Garden not only became the school garden and orchard, but provided space for Robert Taylor Junior to build a beautiful house, so designed by him, to admit as much light as possible from dawn to dusk.

Oh! Also, in my day, the vegetables were not fueled by Miss Thomas' described brew, but by a horse and cart load of good wholesome farmyard manure, tipped in the gate way by Mr. Fred Davies of School Farm, Lower Heath.

CHAPTER 26

June 2010: The Pig

Miss Thomas notes of her school days in the first decade of the 20th century fascinates. Even with the strict undercurrent of utmost discipline under Robert Taylor the headmaster, the scene was tempered with a hive of non-stop activity, all that was needed was to supply input, laced with some enthusiasm. That, Florrie contributed to wholeheartedly, words by her hand bubble with happy memories and she always spoke with pride of having been a pupil of Robert Taylor.

Well, it did leave me somewhat surprised, when she furthered considerable detail about the annual preparation, dispatch and then all the work in preparing the carcass of the schoolmaster's pig, before being cured and then flitches (half a pig lengthwise), and hams hung on the blacksmith made hooks, secured to the beams of whatever room.

Of course, this process was customary for nearly every cottager and household in the Parish. Anyway, it would appear the older boys and girls were involved hands on in this process. Miss Thomas described this scene: "Each Christmas the headmaster had a pig killed, boys and girls had to help catch and rope the pig. The rope was put into the mouth, after much squealing, boys hanging on to its tail and pushing from each side, the pig was moved from the pig sty to the back yard of the school house."

After being dispatched by a little man called Jimmy, we had to roll the pig onto a strong wooden bench. The boys' job was, using boiling water, to scape all the bristles off. After the intestines had been removed and the pig hung on a beam, it was the girls' job to wash and scrape the intestines. This was a terribly cold job, as we had to do it with cold water." Later they had to be plaited, boiled, and then were used for chitling pies – this was similar to mincemeat. As was said: "The only part of a pig that couldn't be used, was the squeal."

Incidentally, the headmaster made no reference to what must have been a very valuable lesson, in the School Log Book. This, coupled with the gardening lessons, were of prime importance for that day, underpinning the basics of life and keeping body and soul together – the killing of a pig and the produce of the garden and orchard. I am tempted to tarry with these lessons, well, with so little money available, "making do," became an art, "frugality out of necessity," was the order of the day and most of it went on within the vicinity of the back door.

There the pig sty, brick built, with its run outlet, beautifully crafted, terracotta pig feeders built into the wall, discharging over a trough to match, all kept scrubbed clean. On occasions even the pig had a bath and would grunt contentedly during the process. Yes, often the pig would become a family pet and as the scales mounted, a familiar sight was to see it on its hind legs leaning on door or wall requiring food or to be stroked and spoilt; especially by the children.

So, come the inevitable day, also brought a welling of tears, "this pig" would walk happily to its place and the dispatcher would comment, "This pig has been marded." Unlike the headmaster's pig which had to be roped, and dragged squealing. This annual cycle enabled relatives and friends to exchange the most-sweetest pieces of pork, as the old folk would say, "You cannot buy that taste today." That taste produced by a happy pig, if only a short life – a pig was only killed when there was a 'r' in the month – aided by ample surplus vegetables, fruit and, of course acorns, another valuable food supply for pigs, whether by forage or collecting by the children.

This, and the inevitable poultry scratching outside the back door, the first meal of that day, breakfast with its bacon, eggs, often mushrooms, gather in abundance before the days of nitrates, was very well catered for. As again, the old folk would say: "A good breakfast put a lining on the stomach and set you up for the day."

Yes, a good breakfast would have been the basic essential for another item mentioned by Miss Thomas in her notes. A May Day treat; being taken by horse drawn lorries to visit the Bury Walls, which was referred to as a former Roman Encampment. Today we know it was an Iron Age Hill Fort. It must have been a very colourful scene as they each carried a bundle of flowers attached to a stick.

CHAPTER 27
July/ August 2010: Be Kind

I think without doubt, our Parish of Fauls was fortunate, and particularly our school, in having two families from stately homes, namely Hawkstone and Sandford, whose commitment to the school and its welfare would last over a total period of one hundred and thirty years. With the decline of the Hill's family fortunes, of which I have written, the Sandford's took up the reins of the school and I had only got to consult Miss Thomas' notes and Robert Taylor's log book entries, plus the old newspaper cutting, to now write about the Sanford family, and especially Sarah Sandford. She, like her husband Thomas Hugh, who died in 1886, fulfilled that commitment to the school until her death in 1916 and she richly deserves mention for her personal contribution of over forty years.

Well! her summer treats went something like this. Mrs. Sarah Sandford gave a treat to the children, numbering at least 160 children, and to their parents. The school was most tastefully decorated with an abundance of flags, wreaths, mottoes, flowers; this work being carried out by pupil teachers, children, and friends. Tea was served to the children at four o'clock and, the rapid disappearance of the good things provided, evidenced their appreciation of the treat. After tea there were games, races, and swings, whilst the adults sat down to an excellent repast in the Infants' Room. Prees Brass Band was in attendance, under the leadership of Mr. Muller, and to their capital music, dancing was indulged in by old and young.

"THERE IS ALWAYS A BOOK ON THE SHELF...!"

All that remained was for the Rev. Harold Burton to propose hearty cheers for Mrs. Sarah Sandford, and thanking her in the name of the school for her continued kindness.

This kindness came again at Christmas time, when Robert Taylor would write: "Mrs. Sarah Sandford distributed presents to all the scholars, also crackers, fruit and mince pies." Miss Thomas wrote: "Every Christmas Mrs. Sandford provided a decorated Christmas Tree, a party and presents which were always practical – red flannel petticoats for the girls and grey woollen socks for the boys." Add to this all the little in between treats she provided for all the children, such as paying for magic lantern shows, one with scenes from the Holy Land, or trips to a visiting circus.

Also, her regular visits to the school, often with her sister or friends, were recorded. During this visit she would look over the boys drawing and the girls knitting and sewing, which seemed to be her specialty. She ran it as a nicely profitable little business, to quote just one extract: "Mrs. Sandford's annual needle work account showed a most satisfactory balance in hand of £2 14s. 11d." She was also the treasurer of the school. Mr. Taylor wrote: "That this committee express their appreciation of the interest which Mrs. Sandford has in many ways evinced in the school."

The final sales of the Hill family estates created a mobility of families; not all tenants wanted or could afford to buy their properties. As a result, numbers of children attending the school dipped over a period of five years before regaining the average. Also, as the emphasis for the support of the school moved from the Hills to the Sandford's, likewise the Sandford tenantry starts to get a mention in Robert Taylor's recordings. Two were Mr. Adams of Sandford Farm and Mr. Higginson of Ashford Garage, both were involved in the management of the school and on odd occasions gave the children treats, with visits to their two properties.

On one occasion the headmaster wrote: "Owing to the kind invitation of Mr. T. W. Higginson, the upper-class boys were admitted to the Agricultural Exhibition of Hedging, Ditching and Ploughing at Ashford Grange, free of charge."

Also, Mr. and Mrs. Adams kindly presented the school with a model of "The Victory" and Miss Thomas wrote: "We were taught to be kind and helpful to people and not expect payment for every little thing we did."

Some of the children from Sandford walked over three miles to the school, some ran along with hoops and a few came on ponies or pony and trap.

Sandford Pupils Meeting to walk to School Together

CHAPTER 28

September 2010: Mrs. Sandford

Life and times are forever moving on, history in the making every day. I love Mary Webb's definition of history, "As a continuation of life into the past." It also permits one to tarry with a certain time and people, in this case of nearly a hundred years ago, it is also within living memory.

So, it is with some pleasure I continue to write about two ladies at either end of the spectrum and their various associations with Lower Heath School, at a period which coincided with the Coronation of George V (22nd June 1911).

Mrs. Sarah Sandford from the stately home of Sandford Hall and Miss Florrie Thomas, whose family had been brick-makers for Hawkstone Estate. Robert Taylor the Headmaster wrote: "Empire Day – In the afternoon Coronation Mugs were presented to the children on behalf of Mrs. Sandford, whose continued ill health is much regretted." At the time she was eighty years old, and in fact, she was never able to visit the school again and she died five years later.

Robert Taylor's last entry in the Log Book about her: "Heard with much regret, that Mrs. Sandford who has been associated with the management of this school since September 29th 1875, died last evening." So ended her wonderful contribution to the welfare of Lower Heath School children and her unflinching support for the headmaster, Robert Taylor.

During those forty years, she had so touched the lives of well over a thousand children, leaving memories of the joy she brought to their early lives, with her kindly influence and treats, in the days when the word treats qualified for its true meaning. Of course, this kindly atmosphere she generated encompassed the Parish as a whole. Where need was necessary, so there was Sarah Sandford, especially with the sick and elderly.

Likewise, as a journalist of that day wrote: "She went about doing good," so touching the hearts of all classes and it was little wonder that country folk and rustic villagers were united in mourning the passing of an old, valued friend. Robert Taylor also wrote: "It would be impossible to detail all the social, religious and charitable organisations with which she was connected, but her association with the Whitchurch Cottage Hospital will stand very prominent." She was Lady President of that institution since its commencement and always took deepest interest in its welfare.

It was Mrs. Sarah Sandford's wish that she be conveyed from her home on a hand hearse. Along the way, at frequent intervals, were seen marks of reverent sympathy and the muffled peals reverberated from Prees Church bell tower. Her last resting place was the family vault which lies under what is known as the Sandford Chapel in St. Chad's Church, Prees, where the light shines in from a most beautiful stained-glass window placed there by this good lady. Sir Richard Sandford was bodyguard to Henry IV at the Battle of Shrewsbury and was killed in 1403. Sir Richard's figure in stained glass, of circa 1434–45, was removed from the windows of Battlefield Church at Shrewsbury and may now be seen in the Sandford Chapel of St Chad's Church at Prees, (sic. Gareth Williams in his book The Counties Houses of Shropshire).

Sarah had also enlarged and renovated the church organ and re-framed the bells and renovation of the belfry, for this beautiful ancient Prees Church.

"THERE IS ALWAYS A BOOK ON THE SHELF...!"

I love one of Miss Thomas' stories, seemingly recited with no less enthusiasm as when it happened some seventy-five years earlier. It was morning playtime, and one of the neighbours came up School Lane with a pony and shandry. On board was a strong store pig under a rope net, bound for sale at Hodnet Auction. However, as they came past the playground, the children all rushed to the hedge to look and this so frightened the horse, it reared. One of the shafts broke, the pig came tumbling out from under the rope net, followed by the farmer on top. The farmer then stood up and said, "Well, Well, Well!" We were delighted, and chased the pig back down the lane, eventually catching and escorting it back to its sty, with some children hanging on to its tail.

She also wrote about the children being allowed the thrill of sliding on the sand hole across the road from the school, where the winter floods and frosts provided a two-acre site of ice. It was the same in my day!

In the Hawkestone Estate Sale Catalogue of 1901, the sand hole was referred to as a very valuable Withy Bed and Miss Thomas said she could just remember the withy (willow) being harvested.

```
                        LOT 53.
        A VALUABLE WITHEY BED AND ARABLE FIELD,
                  Situate at the LOWER HEATH.
  Adjoining the Prees Green and Darliston Road, and occupied by James Dowler and Richard Maddocks,
                      and containing 6·008 acres.
                                                        Quantities.
   No. on Plan.           Description.                    Acres.
                    DOWLER, JAMES.
       2125    Arable    ...    ...    ...    ...         4·098
                    MADDOCKS, RICHARD.
       2128    Withey Bed ...   ...    ...    ...         1·910
                                                  A.      6·008

   The proportions in respect of this Lot of the total outgoings paid in 1900 are as follows :—
          Rectorial Tithe    ...    ...    ...    ...   £0  3  2
          Vicarial Tithe     ...    ...    ...    ...    0  0 11
          Land Tax           ...    ...    ...    ...    0  3  9
              The Timber has been valued at £2 2s. 8d.
```

Hills Estate Lot 53 The Withy Bed and Arable Field

CHAPTER 29
October 2010: Miss Thomas

I am glad Miss Thomas wrote about her experiences at Lower Heath school during the headmastership of Robert Taylor because I know of no other pupil of his, who took the trouble to put pen to paper. So, her observations, sprinkled with anecdotes, provide another window on the times and qualities of Robert Taylor and his school.

Her notes from behind the desk, within the context of her ten years attendance, help to compliment Robert Taylor's marathon of forty-four years, which were only terminated by the introduction of an age limit for teachers' retirement, when he was nearly seventy years old.

Yes, forty-four years of visitations from HMIS and on no occasion did they fault his teaching, drawing on a sample of these reports, (all of which I have read): "This school without reservation still maintains its good name and again passes a highly successful examination in all respects. The headteacher shows he has a good grasp of the work throughout the school and offers useful guidance to the Assistant Teachers."

In all one thousand five hundred children had the benefit of Robert Taylor education, thirty of them became qualified teachers, five of them Headteachers and others became successful in various fields. Some often emigrating usually to Australia or Canada. On 19th July 1911 a Mr T.J. Peat, a former scholar of this school, and now Government Land Agent for Western Australia, called and addressed the children on, "The advantages possessed in the settlements of emigrants to the colony."

At least one of his pupils became a Member of Parliament for the Wrekin Shropshire; Tom Oakley.

CHAPTER 30

December 2010/ January 2011: New Windows

In a government Inspectors report, in which every detail was recorded, I was attracted to the last comments which said: "This is one of the very few schools which still has a tiled floor. It would be a great comfort to children and teachers if the managers could substitute a wooden one."

On the 22nd August 1904, Robert Taylor wrote: "laying of block floor not completed, extension of holidays by one week".

They were referring to the main block of the school that housed all the standards, which had been built by Lady Hill in 1840. But, by now, there were many other aspects the Inspectors strongly objected to. The standards were divided by a curtain, with a stove in the centre of each half, the seating facing the side walls with over 50 children congregated around each stove. The Inspectors recommendations were, that the curtain be replaced by a wooden screen of a folding partition and that the stoves be moved from the centre to the side. All this, plus the requirement of more ventilation and light. On odd occasions, Robert Taylor would write, "so dark this afternoon that work for some time was impossible."

As previously mentioned, these school rooms were the venue for every activity in the Parish for one hundred years. The first thirty of those years, with the curtain drawn back and the

"THERE IS ALWAYS A BOOK ON THE SHELF...!"

seating turned around, it was used for the very well attended church services. Likewise with regular whist drives, followed by dance, pantomimes, and concerts. In 1908 the Vicar of Fauls, the Rev and Mrs. Burton, celebrated their Silver Wedding there. With all this arranging and re-arranging of the school furniture, plus the floor had to be swept, and there was not a caretaker, Robert Taylor paid one of the older boys six shillings a quarter to sweep the floors after school. This was not a success, so he gave two boys the job and, it was a success!

Although by 1902 Government had made grants available for school maintenance, it was not until 1910 that the Inspectors wrote: "It is understood that there are proposals to improve the lighting and ventilation of the classroom, but no proposal to remove the stoves". On September 11th 1911, "re-opened school, attendance good, extension time caused by new windows not being completed."

So, by degrees, and a drip feed of improvement to the fabric of the school over a quarter of a century, HMIS had achieved most of their well-meaning requirements for the school.... just those stoves! But in fairness to the school managers, they had, in that time, built the new Infants Classroom which seemingly drained the Parish of every spare penny.

Miss Thomas did not have the benefit of all that extra light and ventilation, now provided by the huge new windows which are still there today. Having just completed her eleven years at the school. Also, Robert Taylor did not have to make any more entries stating: "Had to send children home early because of the darkness in the classroom."

By Now County Council Sanitary Inspectors were visiting the school and taking samples of water. Miss Thomas wrote: "The water for the school came from a pump in the back kitchen of the school house. The boys had a small porch near to it for their bucket of water, whilst the girls had to carry their bucket of water around to the girl's entry. We were allowed only one bucket full per day and one tin mug for drinking use, which we all used." Many years on, those same drinking facilities were still on offer in my days at school.

But for now, the two large replacement windows, fitted into the eastern wall of Robert Taylor's classroom, must have come with considerable relief to him and his pupils. The two small windows on the western side having been cloaked by the building of the new Infants classroom for the past thirteen years.

CHAPTER 31

February 2011: Winter and Sickness

It was usual procedure at Lower Heath School for scholars to leave school at the end of the term in which they had reached their fourteenth birthday. The exceptions were, if a child had won a scholarship, or left the district and on the very "odd occasion" left early for work at home. The latter of which Robert Taylor, "did not approve," but fully understood the circumstances of some families and the pressure they were under.

Miss Florrie Thomas, who had written so eloquently about her school days, did not fall into any of the above categories. Robert Taylor at the end of her register credentials just wrote, "left February 4th 1909, she was still several months short of her fourteenth birthday". I wondered why, and I think his entries in the school log provided the answer.

29th January 1909; "Attendance very bad this week – whooping cough epidemic", February 5th 1909, "Attendance very bad, sicknesses," and with the same glance, culminating on the 16th February, "Attendance very bad, school closed under medical orders from 17th February to 3rd March."

Of course, winters of that day, with their various illnesses, always took their toll in attendance of staff and pupils. But from December 3rd 1908 to March 5th 1909 was beyond the pale! because of its intensity and duration, with colder weather and snow causing aggravation to whooping cough. In fact, during those three months, all entries referred to illness and many absent, attendance low, bad, very bad or poor, other than, "Collection for Dr. Barnardo's Homes" – £1 8s. 6d. and, "Collection for Lifeboats" – 9s. 1d. All that and there was more. The whooping cough was followed by rose rash and on Miss Thomas' birthday the school was closed through scarlet fever on medical authority.

So, her final months had been swept away by illness, and sad to say she was a "stranger to good health" for the rest of her life. When she wrote her memories of her school days in the evening of her life, she did not mention any of the foregoing illness. I am glad she concentrated on the positives, and that she had enjoyed every minute of the Edwardian school days there was no doubt, and she could not emphasise more, the lifelong appreciation of having received her early education from Mr. Taylor, and these sentiments were forever echoed by her contemporaries.

With my observations on Lower Heath School, I was interested in the Master's entry for 22nd June 1900. The Lord Bishop of Lichfield with Rev. R. Faulkner, and the Rev. H. Burton (Vicar of Fauls) visited. The bishop addressed the children, pointing out the great value of acquiring habits of punctuality, regularity, and attention to duty. Of course, he was echoing the values that Robert Taylor had spent a life time helping children put into practice.

Robert Taylor's bottom line was ultimate discipline, applied in such a way, the children responded, aware of the fact it provided the guidelines to build a better future. They also knew if the odd one stepped out of line, the punishment was available and a second dose when they got home. Robert Taylor always enjoyed and deserved the full confidence and respect of parents and Parish. But of course, there was more and much more and as we know from standard one, life is a

"THERE IS ALWAYS A BOOK ON THE SHELF...!"

two-way thing one only gets out, what one is prepared to put in.

Having scrutinized Robert Taylor's forty-four years as Headmaster, only terminated by an introduced age limit when he was 69 years old, otherwise I am sure he would have gone on until he dropped – such was his "job satisfaction". What were his input ingredients that so rewarded him? I can only try and answer that, by using his own hand. Somewhere during that late 19th century, a young Robert Taylor wrote in the school logbook – I did not make a note of it at the time, but committed it to memory, and now I think how relevant it was. "When teaching children, I find it is very important to cloak facts with interest." Well surely it follows, an interested child is a happy child. Introduce into that a combination of work rate and discipline, hence, qualities that span time.

The whole school was beset with excitement, a dead adder had been found in the grounds. Robert Taylor took the adder into the classroom and gave the children a lesson on it, arresting that excitement and putting it to good use. Just one of many ways Robert Taylor worked his bits of magic. Well teaching is magic ... isn't it? ... it has got to be, I am even excited about it well over a century later.

CHAPTER 32

March 2011: Madge Hocknell

In 1999 Lower Heath School celebrated its bi-centenary. For this wonderful occasion, staff and pupils decided to have the school bell refurbished and re-dedicated – I had never heard it ring in my day. They also came up with the idea of a V.I.P. guest and equally special children to greet her. The school's youngest pupils, four-year-old twins, Emily, and Harriet Grandfield, helped the school's oldest surviving ex-pupil Mrs. Madge Hocknell toll the re-dedicated bell. This task they accomplished with considerable enthusiasm, to the delight of the whole school, Vicar, parents, and friends. Madge Hocknell was also the last surviving pupil of Robert Taylor.

I found it very easy to persuade them to reminisce about their school days, helping to compliment other observations taken on board during my life time, including George Ward with whom I served my time. But, of course, Miss Florrie Thomas was the best, she took the trouble to put pen to paper. In this she was encouraged by Mrs. Bloor, a former headmistress. Whatever their theme was always the same, that they had thoroughly enjoyed the atmosphere generated by Robert Taylor, providing them with the opportunity and encouragement to fulfil their potential at that given point in time.

I love the content of lots of his entries, taken at random: "A plum tree in school garden infested with greenfly, took the opportunity to give the whole school an object lesson on this pest – children much interested."

"THERE IS ALWAYS A BOOK ON THE SHELF...!"

"Children much interested in watching the development of a frog from a tadpole kept in a jar in school window, also silk worms have developed."

"Caterpillars in boxes have developed from pupae eggs which have been laid, children much pleased in watching different stages."

It also appears that Lower Heath swallows arrive ten or twelve days earlier than they did in Robert Taylor's day.

"January 22nd 1901: sang the National Anthem, Her Majesty being very ill. At 10:15pm news of Her Majesty Queen Victoria's death received – school bell tolled; flag hoisted to half-mast."

"June 20th 1902: wet morning – a few infants absent. Dismissed school for one week's holiday Coronation of Edward V11".

"June 30th 1902: re-opened school, addressed children on the illness of King Edward VII and the postponement of the Coronation." In actual fact, Edward had undergone surgery for appendicitis, which for that day was a very serious operation. However, this inconvenience was taken in his stride, like everything else, as was the character of the man and within a few days he was pursuing one of his favourite sports – sailing.

On August 9th 1902 the Coronation of Edward VII and Queen Alexandra did take place and England experienced change. It certainly brought a new dimension to Lower Heath School as Queen Victoria had not been one for celebration but Edward VII was!

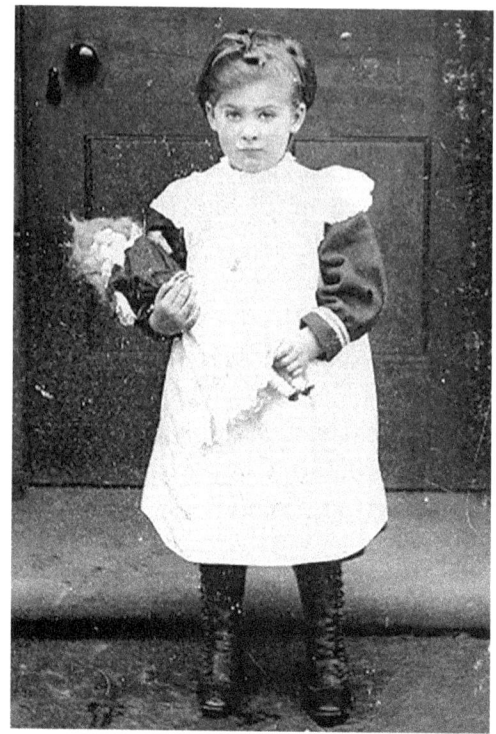

Madge Hockenhall as a School Child

CHAPTER 33
April 2011: Empire Day

Robert Taylor would often record children's reaction to a particular lesson by hand: "Children much interested or very interested." But on 1st March 1900: "children exceedingly interested, heard of the relief of Ladysmith – hoisted Union Jack", then on 21st May 1900 it was really party time, for the relief of Mafeking (both South African provinces).

Rev. H. Burton, as Chairman of Managers, directed that a half day's holiday be granted. Messrs. Higginson and Adams (managers) sent liberal supply of oranges, sweets and nuts, Mr. Higginson being present at the distribution. Things were going well in the Transvaal; it was 2nd June 1902: "Received news of peace being declared. Half day's holiday granted; school dismissed at 12.30p.m. after scholars had sung the National Anthem".

Even a war which did not directly affect us got the treatment – "Lesson given on West Indies to illustrate the Spanish America War – children allowed to read newspaper reports."

On occasion there would be a movement of soldiers, contingents of various regiments passing adjacent to the school when the children were allowed into the road to see them. Of these, a troop of the 17th Lancers passed by one morning at 9.50 a.m. and, for the children, permitted to see them, this would have generated the most interest, even excitement.

Also, at the meet of the Hunt adjacent to the school, children were allowed to leave school to see them. On other occasions, children were allowed to leave school to watch hounds drawing local covers including at Sandford Hall. Bearing in mind, as old George Thomas would say, "When I was a lad, it was mostly woodland around here."

The Hunt Meet at Sandford

There were little treats, dovetailed into the school's routine, fuelling interest. Robert Taylor would occasionally change a lesson for something topical – he gave the children a lesson on the life of W.E. Gladstone, just deceased, and: "Gave the children an account of the sad loss of Scott and his companies in the Antarctic regions."

When Queen Victoria died, Robert Taylor had been headmaster of Lower Heath School for 25 years. He had only once mentioned the Queen's birthday: "May 24th 1900, sang National Anthem and dismissed the school a little earlier,

"THERE IS ALWAYS A BOOK ON THE SHELF...!"

Queen's Birthday"; and that was to be her last birthday as she died 22 January 1901. Well, Victoria was not given to celebrations, but that date was eventually to become very important in the school's calendar.

May 24th 1905: "half day's holiday given as suggested by Education Committee of County Council, for Empire Day. Lesson on the Empire given in the morning and Rev. W.J.B. Hancock addressed children on the Unity of the Empire." It was as if the country had just discovered what a fantastic Empire Queen Victoria had ruled over. To this end the children were made very aware of the many thousands of people, military and otherwise, who had left these shores to acquire and build a vast Empire on which the sun was never to set. So typical entries were: "Empire Day celebrated; instruction given on the British Empire and reasons for the 24th of May being chosen, with patriotic songs and salute of the flag, of which explanation was given".

Yes, the implantation of pride was complete, plus the half days holiday, which only meant for a lot of those children, home, and work, and work provides the basis for any achievement, as instilled by Robert Taylor and hence, the Empire.

This flag hoisting interests me, it seemed to take place at every opportunity, especially where Royalty or Military matters were concerned, whether for joyous or sad occasions.

"Put flag up to half mast – funeral of President McKinley (dies 14th September 1901), explained cause to the children."

On May 7th 1910:" this morning received news of the lamented death of Edward VII, flag hoisted to half-mast".

By now, that flag must have been in a very tatty condition.

July 13th 1911: "in honour of the Investiture of the Prince of Wales, the new school flag (recently presented by Mrs. Sarah Sandford) was hoisted and the children sang 'God Bless the Prince of Wales'" but no mention of flag hoisting a month earlier for the Coronation of George V and I can only assume Mrs. Sandford's new flag did not arrive in time.

CHAPTER 34

May 2011: Grouping of the Standards, Waterloo

On occasions, Robert Taylor would mention a particular lesson, where he would involve all the standards (class levels), which he referred to as the grouping of the standards. For this, it was simple, the dividing curtain between the standards being drawn back, which immediately created interest. The lesson could be about our Empire, anything topical that would span the interest of the children, which was Robert Taylor's aim. But one reason galvanized my attention, which I studied for some time, until everything took on meaning and it was simple.

"Lesson given on Waterloo; whole school involved." Yes, even the infants were dovetailed into Lady Hill's classroom of 1846, to be made aware that this battle being one of the most important in our history to win. Of course, what gave it another very important local dimension was the involvement of the Hill family, where four sons of Sir John Hill fought in the Battles of the Peninsular War, culminating in the Battle of Waterloo, which took place on June 18th 1815.

This particular Waterloo lesson took place on June 16th 1903 at a time when there was an overwhelming wave of sympathy for the Hill family, whose fortunes had completed the full circle. After three and a half centuries as masters of Hawkstone Estates, they were finished.

I have got a beautiful photograph in front of me, taken by Mr. Crosse of Whitchurch of Class IV at Lower Heath School and their teacher Eleanor Taylor; eldest daughter of the Schoolmaster, taken in 1903. There are 35 children on it, all done up in their Sunday best attire, lots of Edwardian lace, even on some of the boys, and ribbons. It was taken outside the headmaster's front door – in present day the entrance to the school office – with its rustic porch and roses, living room on the left and his parlour on the right with its decorative brickwork (now demolished) and a splash of holly hocks. It is a pity that coloured photographs were many years in the future and, also, they did not smile in that day.

School Photo 1903

This photograph belonged to Miss Florrie Thomas who is on it. She had, efficient as ever, written the children's names on the back. A few days before the Waterloo lesson, Robert Taylor had written June 12th, 1903: "attendance excellent. Numbers have increased of late. Highest attendance for many years." So, when Robert Taylor, who taught standards V,

"THERE IS ALWAYS A BOOK ON THE SHELF...!"

VI and VII, drew that curtain back to involve standards I, II, II and IV who were taught by Robert Taylor's two daughters, and Ellis Steventon his nephew. Plus, the infants, usually around 40, in the charge of Mrs. Steventon, (Robert Taylor's sister). I doubt whether there would have been less than 200 children gathered in that classroom – but with the staging system used, children could be packed in.

Most of these children had been the sons and daughters of Lord Hill's tenantry but now represented the last generation of Hawkstone Estate children to attend Lower Heath School. I knew quite a few of these people (especially Miss Thomas) who were never many sentences away from praising the Estate way of life and Lord Hill.

I love Gwen Lewis' (nee Ralphs) description of her family's association with the Estate of which they were very proud of. Her grandfather, was waggoner to Lord Hill, her uncle Ambrose rode postillion on Lord Hill's coach and uncle Albert swept the terrace paths. At Christmas they were provided with a load of coal, a joint of beef and a bolt of cloth, at which her grandmother would stay up all night with the luxury of three candles, turning it into clothes for the children.

The curtain came down on Hawkstone Estates, where many members of the Hill family, both male and female, had contributed so much to the welfare of the local community (and the state in general) for centuries. So, on 16th June, 1903 one curtain came down and the other was drawn back and how better to underline the aforementioned than to mention one of the most brilliant members of the Hill family, General Rowland Lord Hill, who commanded the right-hand flank of the British Army and he was only born a 20-minute sharp walk over the hill from Lower Heath School, at Prees Hall.

Sir Roland Hill

CHAPTER 35

June 2011: Lord Hill, Commander-In-Chief of the British Army

When Robert Taylor, Headmaster of Lower Heath School, delivered that lesson on Waterloo, on the 16th June, 1903, to the whole school, I think it was his way of paying tribute to the Hill family in general, who had built the school and maintained it for its first seventy-five years. He only once mentioned the Hill family again. 19th January, 1904: "Mrs. Burton (Vicar's wife) and the Honourable Miss Hill called and heard the lessons."

Evelyn, who was the daughter of the third Viscount Hill had quite often called in to hear the children read and encourage them. It must have been a very sad time for Evelyn, now living at Fauls Vicarage with the Burtons, having had to leave her birthplace, Hawkstone Hall, which had been built by her family. Now they did not own a single brick of it.

Fauls Green Vicarage Under Construction

But for her wedding on the 28th June, 1905, purely symbolic, she was married from Hawkstone Hall, being the first bride to be married from the Mansion for the past one hundred years and the first daughter born there in two hundred years. The scene was set for one of the greatest days ever experienced by the most picturesque little village of Weston-under-Redcastle, as evidenced by journalists of the day. Also, many years later, a journalist visiting the village to cover a wedding was given an eye witness account of that wonderful day by Miss Symonds, the Hawkstone Estates gamekeeper's daughter.

Owing to the vast popularity of the Hill family, a great amount of interest was taken in this marriage, also Evelyn had endeared herself both to the humblest cottager, and to the largest tenants on Hawkstone Estate, some of whom were part of the 300 invited wedding guests. It was Evelyn's wish to be married at St. Luke's Church, Weston-under-Redcastle (built by her family) and, for this she had to have a special licence. She was given away by her eldest brother, the present fourth Viscount Hill. All floral arrangements were of a lavish scale and decorations in the church were carried out by Messrs. Pritchard & Sons of Shrewsbury.

The scene as the Bride and Bridegroom passed along the covered pathway from the church must have been one of great beauty, and the effect heightened by little children, daintily dressed, strewing the petals of roses and other posies in their path. The ceremony had been conducted by the Rev. Harold Burton, Vicar of Fauls. They progressed from the church, under cascading triumphal arches with appropriate mottoes, erected by the gardeners and employees of Hawkstone Estate.

The reception was held in a huge marquee in front of the former Inn (now Hawkstone Park Hotel), with the floral decorations in the hands of Messrs. Eckford of Wem, and their most sought-after flower of that day in the world, the sweet

"THERE IS ALWAYS A BOOK ON THE SHELF...!"

pea. The village of Weston-under-Redcastle was packed with guests and onlookers, where the high and mighty rubbed shoulders with the humble rustic country folk in their hundreds, all with one accord, to pay respect to the Hill family with their many outpourings of goodwill and not least many a happy tear-stained face.

It is a certain fact, Miss Thomas sitting in on that lesson, extolled the virtues of the Hill family, to my knowledge until her last breath, with the comment: "The Hills gave and gave, till they could give no more."

So, what had been the toast of the Hill family for centuries: "That the Hills would be at Hawkstone, as long as the Hawkstone Hills" was not to be.

The Hill family had been brilliant in creating history, but none more so than on the Battlefields of their day. It must have been of immense interest and pride to the local community to have four members of the Hill family, all brothers, born in the village of Prees, involved in the most important Battle of Waterloo. Three of them were to become Generals and one a Colonel. But it was Rowland, the eldest, who became second in command to the Duke of Wellington and one of his most trusted Generals, who on several strategic occasions covered himself in glory on the battlefields against Napoleonic forces throughout Portugal, Spain, France, and the Plains of Waterloo.

In 1828, when the duke became Prime Minister, Lord Hill became Commander-in-chief of the British Army. Hence the people of Shropshire, of whom many had fought with him, took him to their hearts and subscribed to the erection of Lord Hill's Column in Shrewsbury, one of the tallest Doric columns in the world, standing at 133ft. 6in. (40.69m.) with a 17ft. tall statue of Lord Hill standing on the top of the column. The foundations were constructed before the Battle of Waterloo.

So, what a wealth and quality of local involvement Robert Taylor had at his finger tips to deliver that lesson to the whole school, 88 years after Waterloo.

Lords Hills Column Shrewsbury

"THERE IS ALWAYS A BOOK ON THE SHELF...!"

Lord Hill's Column,
SHREWSBURY.

Erected in honour of Rt. Hon. Rowland Lord Hill, Baron Hill of Almarez, in Spain, and of Hawkestone and Hardwick Grange, Shropshire, G.C.B., Commander-in-Chief of the British Army. Born 1772. Died 1842.

Height of Pedestal	.. ..	13ft. 6in.
,, ,, Shaft and Capital	..	91ft. 6in.
,, ,, Pedestal for the Figure	..	11ft. 6in.
,, ,, the Statue	.. ..	17ft. 0in.
Whole height ..	.. ..	133ft. 6in.
Diameter at Plinth	..	15ft. 0in.
,, ,, Capital	..	11ft. 6in.

TOTAL COST.
Land and Buildings .. £1,955
Column £4,019

£5,974

Foundation Stone laid 27th December, 1814.
Completed 18th June, 1816.

Number of Stones, 326.
Weight of Stones, 1,120 tons.
Staircase has 172 steps.

Cost of Lord Hills Column

General Lord Hill retired in his 70th year, in August 1842 and Queen Victoria made him a Viscount and, after returning to his home, he died on the 10th December 1842.

The country wanted to fete him and bury him in Westminster Abbey, but his Will decreed he would be buried in his own local church at Hadnall, where Hardwick Grange had been his home. In that day Hardwick Estate (since demolished) was owned by the Hill family.

CHAPTER 36

July/August 2011: The Bennetts

I think it must have been a little bit unique for a single family to fill all teaching positions over such a long period of time, as was the case at Lower Heath School, where the headmaster Robert Taylor, his sister Mrs. Steventon (Infants teacher) and their eight children, who each in their turn filled the middle positions as Pupil Teachers. HMIS who were ever ready to sharpen their pencils, not once found fault with the teaching qualities of the school, but on occasions did mention a school of this size really did require another infant teacher.

June 26th, 1907 Certificate list issues results: "Robert W. Steventon (master's nephew) passed with distinction English Language and Literature, History, Geography, Elementary Mathematics and Elementary Science, and Robert B. Taylor (master's son) passed with distinction History and Geography. Both have obtained admission into Saltley Training College."

But two entries by Robert Taylor in the school Log Book signalled the end of this single-family monopoly.

Previously January 7th, 1907, Miss Annie Bennett commenced work as Assistant Mistress. Annie was 43 years old and was to stay in this post until her retirement in 1926. Miss Bennett came with the right pedigree, she and her sister, Keziah, when in their teens, had served a five-year apprenticeship as pupil teachers under Robert Taylor at Lower Heath School. Kezia went on to become Headmistress of a school in Shrewsbury. They were born at Prees Green, where their father was a tailor, and a brother George was now the Postmaster – none of them married.

Misses Annie and Keziah Bennett

Also, on October 1st 1907, Miss Lillian Hyde began work as an uncertificated assistant Mistress, and can be seen on the LH side of the school class photograph found in Chapter 24. Miss Hyde was to stay seven years and was replaced by Mrs. Evans from Sandford. This team, plus the usual pupil teachers, was to take Robert Taylor and his sister Mrs. Steventon through to their well-earned retirement, after 44 years, in 1919.

Just to tarry with Miss Bennett, who appears to have gone about her life and teaching in a quiet sort of way. The Log Book entries would suggest she did not enjoy the best of health, also she cared for her elderly mother till late in her own life. But in the evening of her long life (1864-1955), she took her pen and wrote what she described as: "A few notes on the History of Prees", in a little booklet. Also, she compiled the: "History of Prees Congregational Church" in a Souvenir Programme of 1950 to celebrate the triple Jubilee of the Church, for which she was now Hon. Secretary, a post previously held by her brother George until his death in 1931. Her father, another George Bennett, had been Deacon and Superintendent of the Church for 50 years.

Her last comment in the Programme was: "What the future of our Church will be, it is difficult to say. We can only hope and pray the way will be made clear and that we may go forward and continue our work."

She also wrote in her observations of Prees during her lifetime: "In time the Village people became more enlightened and with the spread of education and the influence of religion, public opinion advanced, licences were refused and the people became more sober in their habits."

So, it must have been of some relief to Robert Taylor to have a ready-made School Mistress, of that quality, on the doorstep to help fill the vacancy left by the departure of the two Roberts previously mentioned, Miss Bennett wrote in her notes: "The school is noted for its excellent management and many scholars, both boys and girls, have been successfully trained in school and college and have occupied positions in the teaching profession and the Civil Service".

Over a hundred years on, even in this "day and age," that little country school is still very much encompassed with those same sentiments.

I was pleasantly surprised recently with conversations I had had with two senior ladies, Mrs. Barbara Hill, and Mrs. Mary Chidlow, who could both remember Miss Bennett very well. Barbara, who was born in 1912, had been a pupil of Miss Bennett and her comments were: "She liked her, she was a good teacher, very strict and would use a cane occasionally – but not on me!" Mary's memories were of racing across Ford Meadow, helter-skelter over a stile through Dick

Johnson's farmyard and her reward, if on time, a ride to school in Miss Bennetts transport, which was a pony and trap driven by her brother George who was the Postmaster at Prees Green.

Prees Green Post Office

CHAPTER 37

September 2011: Retirement Announced

During the last few months of Robert Taylor's marathon 44 years as Headmaster of Lower Heath School, he was able to record the first appearance of Leslie Gordon Sandford Esq. (1866 – 1936). Lesley Gordon was following in the footsteps of Sarah Sandford, who had died in 1916. He, as a manager of the school, was to bring the same endeavour and concern for the welfare of the school children reminiscent of the family. Also, sadly, he was to be the last of a long line of Sandford's who had resided at the Sandford Mansion for over eight centuries, – Thomas 'de Saunford arrived with the Normans and is mentioned in the Doomesday Book. September 27th, 1918, "prizes for the best garden plots were given by Mr. L.G. Sandford Esq. to the gardening classes."

The Rev. R. Stamer, Vicar of Prees, was the judge. The Rev. H.G. Burton addressed the boys saying: "That the donors of the prizes, whose family had been connected with the school for more than forty years, were anxious to encourage the cultivation of the garden plots and were pleased at the way in which the work was done." The Rev. Stamer and Mr. L.G. Sandford Esq. also addressed the class, after which Mrs. Athene Sandford presented the prizes to the successful gardeners. These gardening lessons took place on the last period of the week on Friday afternoon.

During this time the girls were involved in acquiring the delicate, intricate skills of needlework, to which aim they

"THERE IS ALWAYS A BOOK ON THE SHELF...!"

appear to be very good. June 6th 1919: "prizes for needlework were given to the school by Mrs. Athene Sandford. Mrs. Black (of Prees Hall) judged the work and expressed her satisfaction at the results. Mr. L.G. Sandford Esq. addressed the girls, urging them to continue their efforts to become good needlewomen and saying he was glad to receive such an excellent report from Mrs. Black."

Mr. Taylor called for a 'vote of thanks' to Mr. and Mrs. Sandford and to Mrs. Black which was heartily accorded. This was his last entry, of any note in the School Log Book before his final entry.

Robert Taylor's first entry had been on the 29th September, 1875: "School placed under different management. Certified Master – Robert Taylor, Assistant Mistress – Mary Anne Taylor (his sister), Monitors – George Oakley and Elizabeth Moreton, Extra Monitor – John Taylor (his younger brother)" who died young. Robert Taylor made his last entry in the School Log Book on 31st July, 1919. "The Head Teacher Mr. R Taylor, retired under the age limit, Mrs. Steventon, (his sister) Assistant Teacher also retires."

The Rev. H.G. Burton (Vicar of Fauls) chairman of the Managers, addressed the children before the school closed. School closed for the summer vacation – one month and one week as requested by the King George V. So that was it, or was it... not quite.

It was certainly the end of this beautifully detailed period in the history of a little country school, which spanned the last 25 years of the 19th century and the first 19 years of the 20th century. Through the somewhat morbid times of Queen Victoria, the more light hearted reign of Edward VII and the down to earth no-nonsense style of George V, all culminating in that horrible 1914-1918 War which brought Robert Taylor's Headmastership to an end.

Now to turn to the parish magazine of 1919, where the Rev. H. Burton on September 27th wrote: "The presentations to Mr. & Mrs. Taylor and Mrs. Steventon were made in the school. To the fund for this object, the whole parish, and many others, had willingly and generously subscribed. Tea for the school children was provided by the three retiring teachers. We all deeply regret their departure from our midst and wish them every happiness in their new homes."

But it was going to be a long day for them, with the school packed again in the evening, with people laden with goodwill for them.

CHAPTER 38

October 2011: "Behind every good man, there is always a good woman."

Lower Heath School, formerly Industry Hall, had provided the setting for every get together under whatever guise or cloak, for the parishioners of Fauls Parish for 140 years. This time span took place from the building of the school by Sir Richard Hill in 1799 until 1939, when the Rev. Caddick-Adams built Fauls Church Hall and kindly donated it to the Parish in remembrance of his mother.

Goodness knows how many functions had taken place at school but I doubt whether there had been any quite as significant, or as riveting (other than possibly Royalty) as on 27th September, 1919, on the retirement of Robert Taylor the headmaster and his sister Mrs. Steventon.

In the afternoon, the retiring teachers had entertained the children to tea, who were addressed by the Vicar Rev. Harold Burton. At 6.00 p.m. it was the turn of the parishioners and interested parties from further afield, who congregated in considerable numbers to mark the special retirements.

This time it was Mr. L.G. Sandford Esq. who occupied the chair, ably supported by the school managers. Mr. Taylor was presented with a gold watch, a cheque, and an album, containing the names of the numerous subscribers. To Mrs. Steventon a timepiece, a cheque, and an album and to Mrs. Taylor (Robert's wife) a timepiece.

Mr. L.G. Sandford Esq. expressed his pleasure at presiding, more especially as a relative of his, Sir Francis Sandford, when at the Education Department, had signed Mr. Taylor's Teachers Certificate. He dwelt upon the good work which Mr. Taylor had done, and the good example he had set, for which he had the ample testimony of many old scholars and he wished all there, a long and happy period of rest.

Mr. Higginson, as treasurer of the fund, read out the balance sheet. The Rev. Harold Burton, chairman of the managers, then said he had known Mr. Taylor for some thirty six years and could testify absolutely to the excellence of the work done in the school and to Mr. Taylor's straight forward and capable conduct of affairs in educational matters.

Of Mrs. Steventon, he could only say that she deserved the credit in her work as the Infant's Teacher, of having laid a solid foundation for the good work which followed. And, of course, as they say: "Behind every good man, there is always a good woman."

I had noticed on occasions, Mrs. Taylor would sit in on a class in the absence of a teacher, as Rev. Burton said: "Mrs. Taylor in many ways had been a mother to the children in their difficulties and little troubles."

He then presented to each the gifts mentioned. Mr. Taylor, who spoke with some emotion, said: "He could not find words to thank sufficiently, on behalf of all three of them, for the splendid and appropriate presents just handed to them and which they, and their children, would value as they deserved and for the kindly feeling which had prompted the long list of friends, whose names were inscribed in the albums.

Personally, he was sure he did not deserve half the good things which had been said, for he was conscious of many failures

"THERE IS ALWAYS A BOOK ON THE SHELF...!"

and imperfections in his work. But if they had achieved some measure of success, it must have been attributed largely to the excellence of the body of managers who had trusted and helped them in every possible way, to the hearty co-operation and loyalty of their staff of teachers, to the trust reposed in them by the parents, such an important factor in maintaining the discipline of the school and to the especially nice and intelligent class of children whom they had to teach.

He expressed his great pleasure in having the Vicar, still as chairman of the managers and school visitor, and the Squire and Mrs. Athene Sandford having become so interested in the school, thus continuing the family traditions."

Mrs. Steventon briefly expressed her thanks and the meeting ended with cheers and the singing of the National Anthem. Yes, it had been a long day for the Taylors, but there was another important aspect to come.

Mr. and Mrs. Robert Taylor (Senior)

141

CHAPTER 39

November 2011 published December 2011/January 2012: The Great War

Robert Taylor the Headmaster of Lower Heath School wrote in the school log book how interested the children were on hearing about the relief of Ladysmith and of Mafeking. The flag was raised with excitement and a liberal supply of oranges, sweets and nuts were partaken of. However, I have trawled through every entry he made during the 1914-1918 War and can find no direct reference to the War.

The Transvaal was a long way away and I can only identify one soldier who fought in that War, who they would be familiar with – Charles Rowland Hill. He was Colonel of the Royal Welsh Fusiliers and was decorated with the D.S.O. for his services. He became the 6th Viscount in 1924 but this War, in effect in some way, involved everybody. Of the 550 inhabitants (roughly) of Fauls Parish, 81 answered the call to serve in the Great War of 1914-1918, 26 of them paying the supreme sacrifice.

Also, with having a massive Army Training Camp, involving many thousands of soldiers in our backyard at Prees Heath, the whole country side was gripped with an atmosphere of camaraderie and wellbeing. Of course, 1914 saw every available pair of hands involved in the construction of the camp, in fact, most people in some capacity contributed in lots of different ways.

"THERE IS ALWAYS A BOOK ON THE SHELF...!"

Prees Heath Camp Postcard

Winners of the Hut Building Competition for WW1

Hut Builders Family Members WW1

By early 1915 the highways and byways were being pounded by the marching boots of the regiments, always singing away and the bands playing. Their usual destination was Hawkstone Park, which was approached from both the villages of Weston-under-Redcastle and Marchamley.

Weston-under-Redcastle Village (early 1900's photo)

What a contrast, the most beautiful setting of Hawkstone Park, where they enacted their training and manoeuvres, to facilitate them for the awful business that awaited them on the flat bland plains of Flanders, for which in a few short weeks they would embark.

View of Hawkestone Park (photo taken later in 1956 showing Mr. Jack Jones in the foreground)

I have got a photograph of Prees Village in front of me, packed from end to end with marching soldiers of the Highland Light Infantry – we know this by the cap badge – with their band playing.

Prees High Street Highland Light Infantry

I have another photograph which on the back I have written, "Mrs. Allwood of Fauls Farm, with four soldiers off the camp, from the First World War." It was given to me by her granddaughter who said her grandmother frequently entertained soldiers to a meal. It was a gesture of goodwill, practised by many families across the community.

But I like what George Ruscoe wrote: "On Saturday mornings he and his mates – age 10 or 11 – some on bikes, some running behind, would make a bee line for Prees Heath Camp." The excitement of it was still with him 70 years later. Oh! And they managed to "suss" out the friendliest Cook House, where the cook would give them a bully beef or bacon butty to fortify them on their return journey.

The Cook House Prees Heath

Robert Taylor did mention the awful winters of 1916-1917 and hinted he thought absenteeism at times was far more than would account for the usual reasons. Also, that Rev. H. Burton called and addressed the children, with reference to a collection for the serving soldiers, some of which had now been taken prisoner.

"THERE IS ALWAYS A BOOK ON THE SHELF...!"

The Vicar also wrote in the Magazine that he had called a meeting for the purpose of collecting a sum of money to send each soldier of Fauls, a ten-shilling Bank of England note as Christmas present, the same as last year. The Parish responded most generously and the money was posted by registered letter – I notice one of the collectors was Mrs. Allwood.

The Vicar was aware it was yet another burden to put on the Parish, already gripped with sadness and bereavement, which became even more compounded as the despatches arrived from Flanders with their none stop doom and gloom.

But, as Harold Burton said, it was the only way to show appreciation for them. As the Vicar used to say on addressing the school children at every opportunity, "the importance of acquiring habits of punctuality, regularity, and attention to duty." Robert Taylor's pupil Harry Brown acquired all of these and, as a result, won a scholarship to Wem Grammar School. Harry was involved in the Battle of the Somme, survived, and later wrote about his experiences and of friends that did not return. I am glad he did.

Harry wrote with much detail in the form of verse, which I have in front of me. I choose just two of those nine verses.

"At last the day was breaking,
But many did not see.
The daylight nor the sunshine,
There were in eternity.

They bled and died for England,
Their land and homes to save.
And today those lads are sleeping,
In a far-off soldier's grave."

"Lest we forget"

Prees Heath Army Officers 1914-18 War

Prees Heath Mounted Soldiers (Yeomanry) 1914-18 War

"THERE IS ALWAYS A BOOK ON THE SHELF...!"

Soldiers Tobacco Break Prees Heath WWI

Soldiers with Daimler Truck Prees Heath WWI

CHAPTER 40

February 2012: Roger West, Birth

With Robert Taylor's retirement after 44 years as headmaster of Lower Heath School in 1919, 47 years altogether having previously been headmaster of Clive School for 3 years, he had used up his biblical span of three score years and ten. Of course, he was not to know it then, but twenty-two years of retirement (some retirement!) awaited him, completing his life span in his 89th year in 1941. It was so noticeable that Robert Taylor was blessed with the most important jewel of any life, as indeed so was his wife, they both enjoyed good health. In fact, I do not think he was ever absent from the classroom with an ailment of any sort during those 44 years – a most marvellous achievement.

Outside of the classroom, Robert Taylor was a great walker, a very familiar figure tramping the roads and lanes – he would never accept a lift – until age prevented him, only at the very end of his life. He also involved himself in church affairs and was organist at Fauls Church for many years. But his desire to get involved in the welfare of the community was demonstrated immediately he arrived at Lower Heath in 1875.

He started the Lower Heath Cow Club and acted as secretary, until handling the job over to his son Bert, on his retirement. One observer referred to this Cow Club as "the best in the Country." The dire consequences of a cottager or the many smallholders losing their cow, was tantamount to ruination and brought so much distress with it. However, now for a few pence per month and with Robert Taylors organisation, these awful circumstances were alleviated. The Cow Club remained in place throughout the Taylors era of 75 years.

I love the story of the twelve good ladies of Prees and Fauls Parishes who banded together to form a Prees Nursing Association under the presidency of that wonderful, and now elderly lady, Mrs. Sarah Sandford. On her death in 1916, Mrs. Black of Prees Hall followed her as president, who in its 39 years existence, with two meetings every year, only ever missed the odd one or two meetings.

Prees Hall

Only two men were mentioned (apart from the Vicar), Robert Taylor, who was to be the treasurer for 22 years, only retiring from that office when he passed his 80th year; then Mr. Young, headmaster of Prees School took over and the final treasurer was Miss. Taylor, Robert Taylor's daughter, who was now headmistress of St. Giles School in Shrewsbury. In fact, Robert Taylor's wife Mrs. Taylor, his sister Mrs. Steventon, and his sister-in-law Miss Batho from the Mill House Prees, were all founder members.

After a few months, and the initial hard work by collectors and donations received, on 13th November 1909, the Association with the total of £64 18s 0d, felt that would justify them engaging the services of a Nurse and in January 1910, Nurse Ford became the first Village Nurse at a salary of £52 per year. The fees were 3 shillings for a cottager, to be collected half yearly – January and July. Fees for farmers and tradesmen were 5 shillings per annum. After the first twelve months there were 211 members, a healthy bank balance and a grant of 50 shillings was made to the Nurse for coal and a maternity remuneration of 5 shillings per child.

The Association went from strength to strength with their fund-raising activities and, with the increase in fees they were able to take a house in Mill Street for the Nurse. This was furnished at a cost of £35 9s. 7d. defrayed by the proceeds from a rummage sale. Also, other items of furniture were donated, plus a new bicycle which was purchased for her. Her salary was now increased to £100 but so were her duties. She was now appointed as a Health Visitor, also as visiting nurse to Prees and Lower Heath Schools. Her first visit to Lower Heath School was on February 2nd 1914; she was followed by Nurse Ames, whilst Nurse Richardson was to be the longest serving nurse with fourteen years, to whom I am very grateful. She came on her bicycle late one winters night (17th February 1932) to oversee my delivery. My mother always told me that Nurse Richardson said with great authority: "Call him Roger!"

CHAPTER 41

March 2012: Robert Taylor, Retirement

In 1931, Robert Taylor who'd had a period of ill health, resigned as treasurer of Prees Nursing Association in his 81st year. He had been treasurer since its formation 22 years earlier and had guided its finances through to what had now become increasingly more difficult. As the old folk always told us, "You didn't live in the twenties and thirties, you existed" – indeed it was so true. Hence the eternal problem of overheads, with all the endeavours (fund raising events) generated by those good ladies of the Nursing Association on the Vicarage lawns, in the Oddfellows Hall, Robert Taylor's final account was only balanced by a little magic, a grant of £29 0s. 6d. from the County Council.

So, I am glad he retired, because the scene was set for an escalation of expenses, albeit a natural progression for its final 17 years.

Well, in 1935, the bicycle was replaced with a motor car. Then in 1936, what was referred to as a "momentous occasion", an amalgamation with Tilstock took place, who agreed to pay £125 towards the costs. Queens Nurses were now being appointed on a salary of £182, which did eventually rise to £352 per annum. Palmer House in Church Street, Prees was taken over with necessary alterations, plus water mains, electric geyser, and telephone, and in 1940 a new motor car was purchased.

By now the nurse was making well over 4000 visits; subscriptions had been raised to £1 and a bring-and-buy sale brought in just £20. But of course, the grant systems were now firmly in place, where Government, County Council and the Nursing Federation now balanced the books. So, thanks to those wonderful twelve ladies of Prees and Fauls Parishes, plus Mr. Robert Taylor, Mr. Young Headmaster of Prees School, and Vicar Fitzgerald, who had started Prees Nursing Association as we knew it, it came to an end at midnight on the 4th July, 1948 after having served the public faithfully for 39 years.

Oh! I love the story told about the last of the Association Nurses, Nurse Porter. People would say, in a most kindly way, that Nurse Porter seemed to organise her very busy route to drop in at appropriate times where she knew she would be invited to sit down and enjoy a meal, with whoever it was. And so, she would, bless her! Whatever time would she have to cook? Nurse Porter was always quoted as saying that the highlight of her year was her visit to Shrewsbury Flower Show. The last visit of which, she never returned from. What a nice way to depart this world for a very deserving lady, in a very deserving profession.

On Robert Taylors retirement, he and his wife Jane had moved to Heath Villas in Prees, which is next door to the Mill House where Jane had been born. She had been the daughter of Stephen Batho, the Miller, whose family had been millers in Prees back to the 18th century. It was also opposite the Congregational Church where they had been married in 1883. But now Mr. Taylor could indulge in his obvious addiction to walking, walking, ever walking unto his hearts content. It appears for the majority of his now remaining 22 years of retirement, he would walk to Lower Heath School, five days a week, to deliver his son Bert's daily newspaper. He became

"THERE IS ALWAYS A BOOK ON THE SHELF...!"

such a familiar figure tramping the roads, byways, and footpaths, it became a regular saying in the local households: "There's Mr. Taylor walking by."

Heath Villas, Prees Built 1901

So, I was pleased recently, during a conversation with a grand, elderly gentleman, Bill Clorley, who had just reached his 94th birthday said: "I can remember Mr. Taylor very well, the one you write about, I always touched my hat to him and treated him with the utmost respect, as was the custom of that day". He would have been very familiar to Mr. Taylor, having lived in a cottage opposite Heath Villas from 1924. He also described the difficult times of the twenties and thirties as mentioned earlier, but they were still very happy.

So, at 16 years of age, Bill, with no prospect of employment, joined the Royal Air Force. His war service found him a crew member of a Liberator Bomber, involved in some of the longest haul flights of the conflict with the Japanese.

This meant flying from bases in India, attacking enemy installations and railway lines. Of the four gunners on a Liberator, he manned the one in the nose of the aircraft. This position was referred to as the loneliest place on earth. I am sure Robert Taylor would have been quite proud of the little lad who had lived in a cottage just across the road (now demolished) born a son of the family butcher.

CHAPTER 42

April 2012: Prees Hill

I have loved tracking and writing about Robert Taylor, most of the information from his own hand with entries in the School Log Book, of Lower Heath School. Also, many contributions of interesting observations about him from senior citizens – of my younger day – and, of course what other people have written about him. It all adds up to a fascinating bundle, to have brought so much dedication to all aspects of his life, as to become so woven into the fabric of the community, in fact he was a pillar of the community whose door anyone could knock on requiring help.

I know self-motivation is a wonderful ingredient, also to draw inspiration from happenings around one, to be energised and apply it to the benefit of others. This was Robert Taylor, but his determination to walk and walk after his retirement in 1919, in fact he walked to within a few days of his death in 1941, having reached his 90th year.

So, having taught at the school for 44 years, and now retired to Prees, he continued to walk back to the school for most of his retired years, on school days. This continued to furnish his lifelong interest in the school, also now with his son Bert, headmaster, it would have provided a nice family and social occasion. That he delivered his son's daily newspaper, was just "by the way."

He would always use the same route to the school, from his home in Mill Street, Church Street, Prees Wood and Gale

Lane. His return journey, on odd occasions, would be a round trip through Prees Green, but his favourite well beaten track of footpath was through the low-lying meadows of Lower Heath, and the gradual ascent up and over Prees Hill with its various footpath options. Of course, in that day those footpaths were well trodden by people going to the village shopping, also there were always a few Prees children who would attend Lower Heath School including all the Batho family, as it was deemed the best school.

I loved Mrs. Worrall's (nee Jones) comments on showing her a very nice postcard of children sitting at The Tumps, "Oh! Those are the Prees children waiting for a lift on the coal wagon back to Prees." Mr. Taylor, unlike those school children, would never accept a lift in any circumstance. But he would pause and pass the time of day with whoever, and on occasions this was to Mrs. Worrall's granny, who lived in a cottage on top of Prees Hill. They would have plenty in common, both born and lived in the days of the Estate and the Hill family, Granny (nee Pritchard) had been born in the North Lodge where their lives, any time of the day or night had been subject to the cry, "Open the gates," as the members of the Hill Family and staff passed through.

Lower Heath pupils waiting at the Tumps for a Lift Home to Prees on the Coal Wagon

"THERE IS ALWAYS A BOOK ON THE SHELF...!"

Saturday mornings also found Robert Taylor tramping the road, which took him to Sandford Hall, here he administered the first school lessons to the three Sandford daughters, or as Armene, the eldest Sandford daughter put it (who I knew very well): "This tall, bewhiskered gentleman, would come striding up the drive to give us our first school lessons; he was a kindly man, but very strict." These lessons continued until these three girls, each in their turn, went to a private school. He would also teach other children in and out of school activity to play the piano, but I do not know to what degree.

So, Robert Taylor and his addiction for walking, must have taken him over Prees Hill many hundreds of times (walking gives ample time to think) compared with my dozens of times.

I just love, on the odd occasions, to position myself with only the dull, misty outline of the horizon on offer at dawn, then witness the rays of the sun clip the North Staffordshire Hills, Marchamley, Hawkstone, Caradoc, Long Mynd, Long Mountain and the Berwyn Range, bringing the countryside to life all within seconds. Magic!

And, also to think about Prees Hill in a historical aspect, when back in the mists of time, it formed part of an estuary which stretched to Wenlock Edge, the Ancient Britons inhabited the summit of the Hill. The old Roman Road from Viroconium to Whitchurch and Chester came over Prees Hill and between the Church and the Old Vicarage. They also set up shop adjacent. An Anglo-Saxon sword was found in the vicinity and we know they drained the moorland at the bottom of the hill. Also, one of the old Drover roads came over the hill enroute from Wales to Birmingham, but I expect Robert Taylor, the old schoolmaster, knew far more about these things than me.

CHAPTER 43

May 2012: Mr. Robert Taylor, The Final Bell Tolled

In writing about Mr. Robert Taylor, I have often quoted from Miss Florrie Thomas' notes, who wrote with considerable pride at having been a pupil under him. I can easily identify with one of the items she mentioned: "We all had to learn Gray's Elegy;" an elegy written by Thomas Gray in a Country Churchyard, or take on board as many of the nineteen verses they could cope with. Robert Taylor even used it as punishment, privileges withdrawn, until the scholar could recite whatever verses the adjudged misdemeanour warranted. Goodness, it must have been the best punishment ever.

> "The curfew tolls the knell of parting day,
> The lowing herd winds slowly o'er the lea,
> The ploughman homeward plods his weary way,
> And leaves the world to darkness and to me."

The final bell tolled for Robert Taylor on the 1st December, 1941 in his 90th year, after a retirement of 22 years, packed with the same discipline and dedication he had brought to his teaching. Plus, he was blessed with good health to energise his addiction to walking and his other passion, horticulture.

So, I love the story Mrs. Worrall (nee Jones) told, who spent her first twelve months of service, working at the school house. Mr. Taylor would come in, collapse in his chair, hoist his feet, encased in his boots, up onto the hob of the Ironbridge range and within seconds he was fast asleep! What a wonderful

"THERE IS ALWAYS A BOOK ON THE SHELF...!"

way of topping one's batteries up. Well, to walk for most of those years (on school days) to Lower Heath School from his home at Heath Villas in Prees and back over Prees Hill – possibly taking him 70 to 80 minutes, seemed like a marathon to me. Only in the very evening of his life did he exchange this haulage over Prees Hill from which the beautiful changing scenes of the seasons could be seen. I am sure this must have stimulated him on his morning walks, for a more leisurely walk in the afternoons.

These walks took him through Brades Lane and along Pepper Street – denoting an old Roman Road – where the flat fen-like terrain is drained by two streams under the road. Mr. Taylor recorded: "On a good day he would walk to the most distant stream, not so good, the nearer one." This area is also known as Dog Moor, where, on the passing of the 'Enclosure Act,' the good ladies of Prees attacked the Bishop of Chester and his men, the then owner of the lands, and managed to unhorse him, Oh dear! Some of them were put in prison. So, Mr. Taylor, if not walking, as observers would comment, he was busy in his garden amongst his flowers and vegetables and, at-all-times, he was immaculately dressed, otherwise he would be asleep in his chair, or so it appears.

Mr. & Mrs. Taylor's religious tendencies, seemed to be equally divided between the Congregational and Parish churches. Mr. Taylor's funeral service took place at Fauls Church, where he had been the organist for many years, conducted by the Rec. Caddick-Adams and was laid to rest in the churchyard at Prees, he was 89 years old.

His tombstone epitaph reads: "My task accomplished and the long day done." Although they were survived by a son and two daughters, who produced no issue, therefore no grandchildren, there was no door to knock on for bits of additional family history. I felt a bit sad about that.

But as Thomas Gray put it:

> "Now fades the glimmering landscape on the sight,
> And all the air a solemn stillness holds,
> Save where the beetle wheels his droning flight,
> And drowsy tinklings lull the distant fold."

It was the end of the line for the Taylor family, and there were many tributes to him. "One of the best-known figures in Shropshire scholastic circles, many of his pupils going on to find themselves fame at home and in our Colonies."

Of the thirty school teachers he trained, five went on to become head teachers, one a member of Parliament. And almost in the same breath, people would add or write about the Cow Club he formed on becoming headmaster of Lower Heath School in 1875. This endeared him to all factions of the community, underpinning and alleviating anxiety and stress on the loss of a cow.

Likewise, his input into forming Prees Nursing Association. As Colonel Heywood-Lonsdale commented: "Robert Taylor was a great influence for good and of his rule, you can always tell a Lower Heath scholar." He was indeed a pillar of the community, which sat so comfortably on his shoulders. There can never be another Robert Taylor and of course he was a local lad as well. Mrs. Taylor (nee Batho) passed away in her 93rd year, her faculties unimpaired, having been the oldest surviving lady in Prees. She had been connected with all good causes in Prees all her life. Only shortly before her death, she had walked up the hill to Prees Church and attended the Congregational Church opposite Heath Villas where she lived.

CHAPTER 44

June 2017: The Small Holders

To say our 39 local smallholders were very contented "with their lot", a happy go lucky bunch, would be an understatement. It seems once a smallholder, always a smallholder, almost without exception. A couple of them did go on to do other things, one to a farm in Cheshire and another into the sale of animal foods.

All these properties, (except No. 6 which had not been built), were nicely situated in the shadow of Hawkstone Park and belonged to Lord Hill's Estate, at the close of the 19th century. At this time, with the sad demise of Hawkstone Estates, it must have created a lot of anxiety for the smallholder of that day, with the prospect of every property being sold. In fact, three of those smallholders' families, Nos 18, 24 and 38 still live there today. One other family, who bought the land at this time, and later built No.2 are still there.

This provides a nice thread of tenant to owner/occupiers and throughout the 20th century. I am sure this "theme of contentment" filtered through from the early days of Hawkstone Estate.

It was a very well-run Estate, with the welfare of their tenantry very much in mind. In the first Sir Rowland Hill's Day, (he bought the estate in 1556) it was said he had over 1,000 tenants, and never had a missed word with any one of them. He was determined that the son would enjoy his father's farm, that they would have a shirt on their back and bread on the table. Mind you, he was a very wealthy man as apart from his Estates; he was very much into shipping, when trade with the Continent was really taking off. He was also the first Protestant Lord Mayor of London (1549) and it was his descendant Sir Richard Hill (1733-1808) who erected an obelisk in his memory and sat his statue on top of the monument at Hawkstone – with the following inscription at the base: "The righteous shall be held in everlasting remembrance"

Obelisk in Hawkestone Park Sir Rowland Hill

All the ensuing members of the Hill family occupied the same ground with the high ideal for the tenant's welfare and the community in general and country at large.

Of course, the uncertainty and worries caused by the death of the 3rd Viscount Hill Rowland Clegg-Hill (1833 – 1895), and the bankruptcy of the Estate, spread to several hundred families, with the shadow of the impending sales. The two

"THERE IS ALWAYS A BOOK ON THE SHELF...!"

main sales that affected our 33 smallholders were in 1899 and 1901.

The 1899 sale took place on Wednesday, Thursday, and Friday 20th, 21st and 22nd September at, appropriately, the Lord Hill Hotel in Shrewsbury, where 89 properties were offered for sale. At this sale four of our smallholders bought their properties No's 3, 4, 24 and 25. The Auctioneer was F. G. Richards.

The 1901 sale on Monday and Tuesday 17th and 18th June, at the Music Hall, Shrewsbury, where 83 properties were sold, 19 of our smallholders bought their properties; the Auctioneers were Messrs. Hall and Stevenson.

The 10 other properties of our 33, were bought privately before the sales. All this really meant is the properties cost roughly from £350 to £550, they paid 10% down and an interest of 4% on the remainder, instead of paying rent. This is how our 33 smallholders' lives changed, from tenants to owner/occupiers and "all anxiety resolved".

During the 20th century, between 75 and 80 families of smallholders occupied the 39 holdings on Mr. Davies' (himself a small holder at School Farm) list. One of our local smallholders – who got away, so to speak, was George Whitfield who moved from Park Coppice (No. 7) to Norbury in Cheshire to a 60-acre farm. Park Coppice was built in 1908 by Joseph Kirkham. It cost £250 for house, buildings, and drainage; the builder was Richard Powell of Prees.

George and his wife Kate (a local girl from Moat Farm, Fauls) are well worth a mention. Apart from their few milking cows, George made a name for himself of that day, for pioneering the production of deep litter eggs, (some said he was the first). Hens did not lay eggs in the winter months; they just shivered on the perch. So, what George did was brilliant in its simplicity, as he provided shelter so that hens were warm all year round, and the litter used was representative of the hens usual scratching material.

He hung a hurricane lamp in each roost, put in a couple of un-thrashed sheaves of corn and they were in business. Come 12 o'clock at night, the oil and wick spent, hundreds of happy warm, white leghorns would return to the perch. This all caused a terrific interest in the community; people would bike for miles to see the hen roosts floodlit and listen to the crescendo. It was said, in amazement, George Whitfield collected 225 eggs on Christmas morning.

Kate also had the neighbours talking – when her third child gave notice of its arrival, she was milking a cow with a bucket and stool. She withdrew to her bed and Dr. Beckett of Prees duly delivered her son, but, next morning, Kate was back milking the cows! However, with the children coming at regular intervals – pastures new beckoned. The final count of offspring was 8.

PART THREE
Mr. Robert (Bert) Taylor

CHAPTER 45

May 2018: Scots Pines

For the third time, a Robert became Headmaster of Lower Heath School, the last one, always referred to as Bert, and it is through him that I will continue to explore the history of the school up to 1950.

For this I am very grateful to the present Headteacher for the loan of the school log books, with their relative valuable entries of which Bert made 1,779, hearsay still available and first-hand observations of my own. He was my headmaster and always carried my utmost respect.

This headmaster, like previous masters, lived in the school house, or over the shop as they say and Mrs. Taylor was the caretaker of the school, which was up for hire for all the communities' activities, which were considerable in that day. When the school managers met, up to the minute accounts were presented, they having set the scale of charges; 15/– for the whole school, 10/– for the large room, now the Gym, 5/– for the infant's room, and it was agreed unanimously that the new piano would be free of charge. Also, on dancing nights, the participants were requested to move the desks to the sides and replace them after brushing the block floor.

So, the new headmaster soon established his personal identity on the school and the observations of the first visit from HMIS Officer must have been very satisfying and encouraging for him and his staff. He was certainly very pleased with the new piano and equipment suitable for organised games.

"The senior children are capably taught by the headmaster; they are being successfully trained to study independently and the systematic preparation and supervision of the work of these children promises results of a very creditable standard."

But it is fair to say, Bert had inherited several good teachers from his father, two of which were Mrs. Evans from Sandford and Miss Bennet from Prees Green, who had recently handed in her resignation on completing thirty years – qualifying time for her pension – and was then re-engaged as an uncertificated teacher. She was to teach for another six years. The HMIS referred to these teachers as very conscientious, trustworthy and are benefiting from the new methods of teaching, of which teachers from other schools were now coming to observe, giving a nice boost for the headmaster, his staff, and Lower Heath School. On 22nd February, 1923 the schoolmaster wrote in the Log Book: "Captain Kewley (a member of the Committee of Managers) died, arrangements for a floral tribute to be sent from scholars and staff."

Capt. Kewley was very popular and involved himself in all aspect of benefit to the community, and was a founder member of the Prees Branch of The Royal British Legion and it was said of him he had been in the thick of it during the 1914–1918 War and he was to lose his life in a very unfortunate manner. Capt. Kewley lived at Heathgates Farm and was in the process of planting six rows of Scots Pines down the right-hand side of the drive and was returning from Prees Station, having collected the last load in his car, when he was involved in an accident with a horse drawn vehicle.

"THERE IS ALWAYS A BOOK ON THE SHELF...!"

Prees Station

Prees Station Staff

The roads and highways having been the domain of the horse for all types of transport, were now being invaded by these smelly boxes on wheels, to which they took strong objection. So having met suddenly on a bend, the horse startled, and reared, breaking one of the shafts, which on its downward plunge entered the chest of Capt. Kewley, causing his death. He was laid to rest in Fauls Churchyard.

With the passage of time, I counted 96 of those Scots Pines remaining, providing a wonderful landmark and the canopy occupied by a very busy, noisy Rookery or per the Oxford Dictionary: "a group of trees in which rooks have built their nests."

CHAPTER 46

June 2018: The British Legion Shield

As we know, there are always a few people who work hard behind the scenes, under whatever banner, helping to bring aid, goodwill in promoting the community spirit and to this aim after the 1914/18 War, another very important body was formed – The Royal British Legion.

On the 5th July 1924, Mr. Bert Taylor wrote in the School Log Book: "British Legion (Prees Branch) Athletic Sports, held at Prees." Teams representing local schools competed for the Challenge Shield; our team did exceptionally well, winning by a good margin. In fact, those Legion Annual Sports were to become very prestigious and a must, with seniors also competing, drawing in crowds from all around the area, plus all the usual sideshows.

Mr. Bert Taylor was to bring that bit of extra emphasis to sport with his scholars and later in the decade, he was able to write: "The School Sports Team won the British Legion Shield for the third time in succession, and it becomes the schools permanently." It was obviously a very proud occasion for the school and the 15 members of the winning team, as their photograph depicts, with Nellie Stobbart sitting on a chair in the centre holding the shield, which is still polished up and put on display by the school today.

The Winning Team

This recalls a nice story conveyed to me by Nellie Stobbart's two sisters, Mary, and Lilian (Nellie now passed away), who were the daughters of the Head Gardener at Sandford Hall. Nellie had a spell of being niggly, irritable, crying, not wanting to go to school, so Dad sent for Dr. Beckett and after two visits he said: "Mr. Stobbart I can find nothing medically wrong with your daughter, I will not come again." So, Dad made her stand outside in a morning and poured a watering can of water over her, which very soon provided a cure, and she was to become one of the schools' best athletes in track and field events between the two Wars.

Mr. and Mrs. Stobbart House with their four children (Head Gardner at Sandford Hall)

"THERE IS ALWAYS A BOOK ON THE SHELF...!"

The school now having won the shield four times in six years, Mr. Bert Taylor recorded how the girls had also taken the prizes for their baskets of wild flower displays, one of which was Kate Ridgway, who became Mrs. Kate Williams, who having been taught to play the piano by Mr. Bert Taylor, became Fauls Church organist for 50 years.

Kath Williams Organist at Fauls Church for 50 years

The school under Bert Taylor's headship was proving to be a very contented and happy ship, very little punishment recorded, attendance levels frequently recorded at over 90% present for such and such a month, very good HMIS reports. The one treat the children really enjoyed was the school fete, especially on the occasions when they took place in the grounds of the stately home of Sandford Hall, invited by Squire and Mrs. Athene Sandford, who also relished the opportunity to entertain the children.

I loved the story related to me by the late Tom Bloor, who recalling these views of past pleasures, also mentioned the excitement generated when he, and several other children, were invited to see a swallow's nest with young in. It was built between the wall and wardrobe in one of the bedrooms at Sandford Hall.

It was brought to the notice of the whole school, that an old scholar of the school, Mr. Tom Oakley had been returned as Member of Parliament for the Wrekin division of Shropshire and a telegram of congratulations had been sent from staff and scholars. Also, the Rev. Harold Burton urged the children to strive to uphold the reputation of the school, emphasising Mr. Tom Oakley's achievement, who later called and presented the school with a framed photograph of himself.

Empire days were always celebrated, giving the Rev. Burton another opportunity to address the scholars on its meaning and urging them to follow the examples of The Royal Family. Holidays were given for the wedding of Princess Mary (1922) and the marriage of the Duke of York (1923).

However, I liked the log book entry: "Headmaster absent, attending a conference on singing at Wem C. of E. School." This was a follow up of HMIS expressing a desire to develop music throughout the County schools on being impressed on hearing the Lower Heath children sing.

CHAPTER 47

July/August 2018: Miss Annie Active

As Bert Taylor approached his first decade as Headmaster of Lower Heath School, he must have been well pleased as he transferred the content of HMIS's Report into the School Log Book, which was always produced at the School Managers Meetings.

Now, as I look over his shoulder 90 years on, I know he came with an impeccable reference and, most importantly, he had now proved he was able to take on board the art and skills of being a Headmaster, in communicating with his scholars in helping them achieve their best, in the most important pursuit of their education. "The school continues to progress under the quiet direction of the headmaster, assisted by a hard-working staff. There is a pleasant tone throughout and the scholars show both interest and industry. The headmaster has shown initiative in the reorganisation of the school into junior and senior divisions. The physical needs of the children receive careful attention and stimulus is given through team games, all typifies the overall report, underlined by the encouragement of constant revision."

On the 30th August 1926, Miss Annie Bennett terminated her long-term association with the school, as a scholar, pupil teacher and assistant teacher. At the close of school, Mr. Robert Taylor (retired Headteacher of this school), the staff and scholars presented a leather writing case to Miss Bennett and expressing the wish she may enjoy many years of retirement. And she did!

The vacancy caused by Miss Annie Bennett's retirement was filled by another Annie, Miss Active, who commenced her duties on the 1st October 1926, as an Uncertificated Teacher of Standards 3 and 4. Miss Active's appointment by the school managers was to be very significant, in that she was to become the third longest serving teacher in the history of the school, after Mr. Robert Taylor (Headmaster) and Mrs. Steventon (Infants Teacher) who both retired due to Government regulation after 49 years.

Miss Active had just left Wellington High School for girls at the age of 18, had travelled for her interview on her bike, from her home in the little hamlet of Rushden, situated at the western foot of The Wrekin. In the evening of her life, 60 years on, I had the pleasure of taking her on a nostalgic journey back to her birthplace and area, which gave her the opportunity to enthusiastically reminisce and likewise for me to listen. Here her father had been employed on the local Estate, which had also been the birthplace of Mary Webb, whose novels and poetry about Shropshire country folk Miss Active was very well-versed in.

The area was idyllic, the spires of Shrewsbury as a backcloth, the River Severn meandering through the flood plain, in the days when the hedgerows and verges had been awash with wildflowers, plus she had lived through that horrible 1914/18 War and had been subject to a very strict upbringing. All influences that were to enable her to bring the necessary qualities to the classroom, which complimented the Taylor regime and she was to be responsible for teaching, by her own estimate, well over 2000 children in her long stay.

However, she did not get off to a good start; in her early days she overheard children in the playground referring to her as, "Owd Annie." She said, "I sobbed into my pillow all night."

Then a few days later I heard them referring to Mr. Bert Taylor, the Headmaster as 'Owd Bert,' it never bothered me again, what I overheard in the playground."

I was to become one of those 2000 children she taught (but not yet born) and later will visit the influence she was to bring to me, and many of those other children during her 40 years of teaching Lower Heath School children.

Teachers Miss Annie Active RH side (Miss Hanley centre)

CHAPTER 48

September 2018: Rev. Caddick Adams

For Lower Heath Church of England School, the 1920's were seemingly packed with activity, happenings, and providing a wonderful focal point for the community in the Parish of Fauls. Indeed, as it had been since its inception in 1799. It was certainly a wonderful foresight by Dame Mary Hill to build a school on the waste lands of Lower Heath, to which she contributed in her will, and it being the first school of its type to be built in Shropshire.

So, on the death of the 5th Viscount Hill, Francis William Clegg-Hill (1866 – 1924), who had been a Trustee of the school for many years, a letter of condolence was sent to the Hawkstone family by the school managers, mentioning the generosity of the Hawkstone Hill family to local education, to which the Dame Mary (for poor children) Charity helped with the upkeep of the school until the charity closed in 2018 (sic Charity Commission for England and Wales).

On 8th July 1927, the school was closed, and in the afternoon the scholars and staff were assembled for the occasion of the retirement of Rev. Harold and Mrs. Burton who were leaving Fauls Parish after 44 years. The Headteacher, Mr. Bert Taylor, in presenting Rev. Burton with a fountain pen from staff and scholars, referred to his 44 years association with the school as Chairman of Managers and correspondent. He thanked him for all the work involved and his, "never-failing interest and support."

"THERE IS ALWAYS A BOOK ON THE SHELF...!"

Mr. Burton in his thanks gave an inspiring address and a vote of thanks was proposed for his hospitality by Ted Oakley, Esq. M.P. (an old boy) and seconded by the Headteacher, with the children giving hearty cheers.

But then, and most importantly, the children were "treated" to a wonderful tea, by the retiring Vicar and his wife.

The Burtons, who were natives of Lincolnshire, came in 1883 to the scattered Parish of Fauls, the Reverend, having been educated at Oxford, "fell in love with the Faul's people" (his own words) and never ever wanted to leave, both becoming very hands on, and an integral part of our Parish. On Sundays, in that day, most of the time for Lower Heath scholars was taken up by church services and Sunday School, "toing and froing" to Faul's Church and the two local Chapels of Prees Green and Darliston.

At Fauls, Mrs. Burton brought a lot of enthusiasm as choir mistress; she must have been well pleased, as most of her choir were current or ex Lower Heath School pupils who were well steeped in the Taylor's ethic of singing and, of course, Methodists need no encouragement to sing.

Here, my thoughts now dwell on a story conveyed to me by George Mellor.

As a youngster of that day, you had to be crafty. Sunday school was held in the mornings at Darliston Methodist Chapel and at Fauls Green Church in the afternoons. We could fit them both in and qualify for, "two lots of treats." So, whether it was games on the lawns at Fauls Farm, with the two Miss Allwood's and Mr. Forrester who ran the Darliston Sunday School or likewise at the Vicarage with the Vicar, his wife, and Mrs. Athene Sandford their Sunday afternoon school teacher, and of course access to the well laden tables of food and drink at both locations!

When the Rev. Caddick Adams took over from the Rev. Burton, he was heard to ponder: "How can you be in the R.A.F. in the morning and in the Army in the afternoon"?

Simple, if a treat was involved, in the day when a treat was a TREAT and what did denomination mean anyway!

Darliston Chapel

The Rev. Caddick Adams, a bachelor, educated at Oxford, was a kindly, devoted vicar and brilliant pianist and like the Rev Burton, he was to spend all his working life as Vicar of Fauls living in the Vicarage, (apart from his curacy years, which were spent in Australia). He was a regular caller at Lower Heath School, arriving first thing on Monday mornings to check the register. Although he owned a Rover car, he was regularly seen circumnavigating his Parish on his bicycle with his dog Tojo chasing behind. He had been a native of Stoke-on-Trent.

"THERE IS ALWAYS A BOOK ON THE SHELF...!"

Fauls Green Vicarage Side Elevation

CHAPTER 49

October 2018: Oliver Dutton

As mentioned, Lower Heath School being the vibrant hub of the community with so much activity, but there was one happening which was to be very special, and it arrested the attention of all the powers that be, and local press. All were gathered to celebrate a unique occasion. This was a presentation to George Oliver Dutton – known as Oliver – who had never missed a day of attendance throughout his school life; a most remarkable record with much credit being paid to the lad and his parents.

Squire. Sandford, Chairman of the School Managers, heartily congratulated the boy on his magnificent record, which had brought such credit to himself and the school. He then made the presentation of two volumes of "Wonder Books" each being inscribed: "Presented by the Managers of Lower Heath School to Oliver Dutton in recognition of his highly credible record of perfect attendance." Also, the Managers granted a half-day holiday to the school, in honour of the attendance record of George Oliver Dutton.

I knew Oliver Dutton very well, through his evening years, and he loved to reminisce about his school days and of his wonderful record. He told me: "Roger, it was not quite true, there was one Monday morning I was absent for three hours, when I had to attend Whitchurch Magistrates Court, having been a witness to someone stealing milk from a smallholder's churn on several occasions." "Also, my dad, who was the local postman, was a very amiable, hale and hearty, well met

"THERE IS ALWAYS A BOOK ON THE SHELF...!"

gentleman but he was very partial to a few glasses of beer and often, one was better off at school than at home!"

Lillian Mellor, who left Lower Heath School the same day as Oliver – both she and Oliver were members of Darliston Sunday School – loved to share her thoughts from memory lane. How they managed to pack over a hundred people into that little Chapel for special occasions I will never know. There would be two dozen of us youngsters, in our white blouses and shirts, shoulder to shoulder, sitting cross legged on the carpet and we loved it when Mr. Venebles came to preach. We were all ready to count how many times he would say, "My dear friends," would it be 30, 40, 50 or 60 times, and his story of: "Our postman, he comes to the wicket singing away at the top of his voice and you can still hear him singing away in the distance, if only there were more people in the world like our postman."

Mr. Arthur Venebles, with his brother and two sisters farmed Broadhay Farm, and none of them married. They were a very kindly family, and Arthur was a very devoted Methodist Preacher. His mode of transport was a sit-up-and-beg lady's bicycle.

Oliver's attendance at Lower Heath School spanned the years from 2nd June 1919 to 2nd August 1928 during which he sang in the school choir and was a member of the Athletics Team that had been so successful in the British Legion Sports Day. He won an Empire Medal, for his essay and was to pursue all with dedication for the rest of his life, becoming a very much respected member of the community. To the best of my knowledge, with the help of his cousin Janet Dutton, Oliver worked for The Salopian Cattle Bowl Co. – an engineering company which eventually become Rubery Owen – all his life. On his marriage to Doris, they were the first occupiers of Park Terrace, Prees, where they both remained for the rest of their lives. Oliver had been a member of Prees Fire Brigade, a Special Constable, and a very enthusiastic committee member of Prees Amateur Football Club. He also loved coming to Lower Heath School to help teach the children with their Cycling Proficiency lessons and talk about his school days there.

Oliver was always proud of the fact he had been a pupil at Lower Heath School and been taught by the Taylors, also of being a member of first Darliston and then Prees Methodist Church, where he compered, with May Gleave, their very popular Annual Concerts and unlike his father George, he never touched a drop of alcohol. However, on balance, Olivers dad George, the singing postman, who I can just remember, had done his duty with his four brothers on the Battlefields of Flanders. Two of his brothers never returned and George sustained a very bad leg wound which impaired him for the rest of his life. Dedication comes in many ways.

CHAPTER 50

November, 2018: The Sandford Brothers

Sidney Jones, a small holder at Prees Wood, related to me the sad story of his school teacher Jane Morrey, who on a day's sail out of Liverpool, lost her life when her ship, the S.S. Hesperian, was torpedoed by a German submarine. Jane, who was a Prees girl, was on her way to marry her Canadian soldier boyfriend.

The German submarines had been much cause for concern, creating havoc with our shipping lines, launching their attacks from the comparatively safe-haven of Zeebrugge. Heads had rolled. Something had got to be done. This was to involve a massive Royal Naval operation, which helped to hasten the end of that horrible hostility that was the 1914-1918 War.

My train of thought now takes me to Sandford and the Sandford family, a family whose name had decorated the Battle Rolls of England for centuries. Mrs. Morrison (nee Sandford, now passed on) kindly gave me details, of which she was very proud, and rightly so, of the exploits of her two cousins Francis and Richard, who were very much involved in the above-mentioned operations. So, it is with their personal involvements, which now permits me to progress this article.

It fell to Lieutenant R. D. Sandford (Richard), the youngest brother, to command a submarine with a crew of three on an H.M.S. C.3. This submarine was packed with T.N.T. Their mission, to blow up what was referred to as the Zeebrugge mole, a mile-long seawall jutting into the North Sea, studded with machine gun posts and artillery gun positions, right under the noses of the German defences which were massive. Richard could have used the 'Gyra' steering gear, exiting the submarine which would have been comparatively safe for him. This he disdained and preferred, to make sure by placing the vessel in position himself, between the piles and installations of the viaducts, before lighting the fuse and abandoning the submarine. Richard was picked up, severely wounded, and later awarded the V.C. (Victoria Cross)

It was Richard's elder brother, Captain F.H. Sandford (Francis) D.S.O. (Distinguished Medal), R.N. (Royal Navy) who was responsible for planning the above venture and for rescuing the crew of the C3. Francis was well qualified for this job, having already served in the Dardanelles, where he was severely wounded, mentioned in dispatches, and was decorated with his D.S.O. He had also carried out attacks on mine fields and other fortifications. So, it was recorded as invaluable, the preparations he carried out and demolition arrangements in fitting out the submarine C3. and the whole attack in general. He carried out the rescue of the crew of the C3 by means of a service picket-boat, in which he covered 170 miles during the voyage to and from the Belgian coast. For his services in the raids, which closed the harbours at Zeebrugge and Ostend, he was promoted to Commander R.N. and received the French Croix-de-Guerre with Palm. This is an award made by the French government for French and allied troops cited for bravery, and by the addition of the Palm it meant they had been mentioned in army dispatches.

His achievements were recorded in the London Gazette on the 21st May, 1918. I have a photograph in front of me of Richard and Francis Sandford leaving Buckingham Palace, where Richard had been decorated with the Victoria Cross by King

"THERE IS ALWAYS A BOOK ON THE SHELF...!"

George V, for what was described as an "Immortal exploit" on St. George's Day, 23rd April, 1918 by blowing up the mole at Zeebrugge and, within six months, that horrible Great War was over.

Richard and Francis departing Buckingham Palace after Richard received the Victoria Cross; Extract Zeebrugge Mole Exploit (Tablet placed at Zeebrugge); Francis' Obituary London Gazette 1926

The Ruins of Zeebrugge

But sadly, also was the life of Richard, who died on November 23rd 1918, of typhoid fever. He is remembered at Zeebrugge by a Tablet which was unveiled by a member of his crew as a, "Tribute to the Heroic Commander of Submarine C3."

Francis was promoted to Captain and became Assistant Director of the Plans Division of the Naval Staff. But he too had an unfortunate demise; he died at Wengen, Switzerland of blood poisoning at the age of 38 in 1926.

Sidney Jones' sadness at losing his school teacher, Jane Morrey, was still uppermost in his thoughts to the last day of his long life. I do not suppose he ever knew of the involvement of those Sandford lads, whose family had only lived a few fields from him, but I am glad I do, for it is good to know and remember the sacrifices people have made for their Country with their lives and limbs – and still do today.

"Lest we forget"

CHAPTER 51

December, 2018/January, 2019: Late Night Dancing

Being aware of all the business that took place with schooling, out of school activities, all social events of the Parish, meetings in all their various forms that enjoyed the facilities of Lower Heath School, gave me pause for thought. I know the managers of the school, usually the local Squire (as in this case) and a few dedicated people who gave their time to this aim, who were responsible to the Education Department of Salop County Council based at the Old Shirehall Shrewsbury. But pivotal to all this, the most important person was the Headmaster, Mr. Bert Taylor and of course his wife, who was the caretaker of the school, and living on the premises in the school house, and it was a twenty-four-seven job for them both.

After seven years in the job as caretaker, Mrs. Taylor – who I do not think enjoyed good health – resigned, having taken the job over from her mother-in-law Mrs. Taylor Senior, for the sum of £18 per annum.

I am amazed at the volume of work involved in running the school, apart from the most important job of educating on average about 130 – 140 youngsters, and very importantly, in those winters, they all had to be kept warm. The only means of heating the school premises were coal fires and two huge stoves, with all that early morning preparation and maintenance of temperatures throughout the day, and for evening activities, as heating and lighting paraffin lamps was part of the rental fees, it was a busy job for the caretaker.

Mr. Bert Taylor, in addition to recording the details and progress of the children's education in the beautifully kept school log book, also wrote up the Minutes of the School Managers Quarterly Meetings, concerning the business and running of the school, most items on their agenda already highlighted by his Report. First, always accounts, balance, current and deposit, bills cleared for payment and the seemingly never-ending fabric requirements – interior, exterior grounds, fencing, girls' and boys' offices and toilets, all in their turn needing attention.

Then the solutions, and often the Headteacher was requested, authorised, or directed to approach the local trades personnel to attend to whatever parcel of work was required. However, the two parts I liked best were, firstly, the little playground was subject to flooding, and Mr. Bert Taylor was to arrange for it to be drained into the lane and, if possible, not to cost more than five shillings. Secondly, the roof light over the big room had forever leaked, so payment was withheld for the latest attempt to cure it. When, Mr. Taylor drew it to the attention of the school Architect, the solution was simple, take it out and slate it over!

On two occasions Mr. Bert Taylor wanted improvements to the school house. He was asked to get estimates and any cost over £10 and £5 must be defrayed by himself or have 10/– added to his rent per annum. When the Headteacher paid his annual rent, it was less the cost of minor repairs paid for by himself and usually leaving a balance of seven or eight pounds due to the Managers account. Overall, the ongoing business of the school was very balanced, by no means self-supporting, the bigger bills i.e. painting and decorating being

"THERE IS ALWAYS A BOOK ON THE SHELF...!"

funded by the Education Department but the school managers always had to find part of the cost.

So, on the resignation of Mrs. Taylor as caretaker, it was decided to raise the present charges for the school hire to the following amounts. The whole school £11s.0d. the large room 15s. 0d. and a portion of the large room or infant's room 12s. 6d. Also, one of the smaller rooms was to be let at a cost of 5s 0d. but not to be occupied for more than two hours. All fees to include heating and lighting and the Caretakers fees to remain as arranged in 1910.

The only free use of the premises was given to the organisers of Whist Drives, followed by a dance in aid of The Red Cross and Prees Nursing Association, but, with the firm emphasis, "they did not approve of late-night dancing at the school." Also, smoking was not allowed at the school if the children were in class the next day.

Oh! there was still no charge for the piano and it was noted that the cost of coal to heat the room for the Sunday School, was estimated at 3s. 6d. a quarter.

CHAPTER 52
February, 2019: Sing

I think Mr. Bert Taylor could be well pleased with the progress of Lower Heath School under his leadership over the first dozen years or so, all recorded by his own hand, which permits me to meander between the lines and gauge the quality of atmosphere in which his teaching skills were delivered.

Well, it was certainly a winning atmosphere, the school's athletes having won the British Legion Shield on (now) five occasions and the 25 members of the School Choir had done very well in the Schools Musical Festivals at Whitchurch, also very favourable HMIS reports, which referred to the kindly dedicated staff Mr. Bert Taylor had working with him.

This instigates my thoughts to dwell on one of those teachers Mrs. Evans, a name I have heard mentioned so many times from senior citizens reminiscing about their school days at Lower Heath School. Mrs. Evans was the Infants Teacher from 1916 to 1932, and she appeared able to dispense the required disciplines of teaching, so cloaked with love and kindness (two of the most important ingredients in life) that was to endear her to her charges, who never forgot her. Tapping that reminising, it appears Darliston children, on their way to school, would congregate outside Miss Weston's Shop and wait for the Sandford contingent of school children, who would be coming across the fields with Mrs. Evans, hand-in-hand with a couple of her youngsters.

"THERE IS ALWAYS A BOOK ON THE SHELF...!"

Darliston Post Office (Miss Weston centre, her mother RH side, and Miss Ford LH side)

I also loved the reminiscing about Mrs. Evans by Mrs. Hockenhull (nee Maggie Lightfoot) who lived at Ford Farm, Darliston in her infant days: "Mrs. Evans was the eldest daughter of the Sandford Gamekeeper and quite a robust young lady, who would hoist me up onto her shoulders and carry me to school."

And so, the children came in groups, all on foot, from Mickley, Fauls and beyond, who would come down Yew Tree Lane and join with the Marchamley Wood children and then progress along Lady Hill's Coach Drive to school. The Nook Lane children would follow the footpaths over the fields and through the woods on to Lower Heath straight, joining with the Prees Green children.

*Nook Lane Path through Lower Heath Woods
to join Lower Heath Straight*

However, by 1931 a few bicycles started to appear, with children from the outlying reaches, and in 1932 the Managers decided they had got to provide a bicycle shed for the boys – which must not cost more than £5. For the girl's cycles, a share of Lady Hill's Coach House, which was built in the middle of the 19th century and holding all the school gardening tackle would answer the need. Very pleasing to the Managers as it was at no extra cost! They had applied to the Education Authority for help with the £5 for the boy's bike shed, without positive response, for it was the days when thrift was exercised to the ultimate; however, there was one occasion it was taking a bridge too far.

The Managers had instructed the headmaster to approach four builders for estimates for the disused galleries in the Infants Room to be removed, which had originally been used in the days of the old Industry Hall Classroom. But several years later they were still there, much to the displeasure of

"THERE IS ALWAYS A BOOK ON THE SHELF...!"

HMIS who wrote, "They were wasting space" and he didn't like the heavy desks the children were sitting at. The galleries were taken out – one can still see where they were anchored to the walls – and the desks were advertised for sale, all replaced by tables and chairs.

What was well documented was how generous the School Managers were in contributing £1 1s. 0d. to the cost of conveying the 25 members of the School Choir to the Whitchurch Music Festival. Also, I loved the log book entry: "School closed all day owing to necessary preparations for the school concert at night." This was a great success and the proceeds not only defrayed the Christmas Party for the scholars, but there was a healthy balance left for the sports fund as well. Only for me to add, Mr. Bert Taylors emphasis on getting those children to sing and participate in sport; how he must have enjoyed the fruits of his endeavours.

Oh! I know of only one pupil left who had been taught by Mrs. Evans, Mrs. Doreen Dodd of New Farm, Fauls, who has just celebrated her 95th birthday (who at the time of editing has reached over 100 years), a nicer, kinder lady one could ever wish to meet, just like her first teacher, Mrs. Evans.

CHAPTER 53

March, 2019: National Savings

Following the resignation of Mrs. Taylor, the new caretaker of Lower Heath School was Mr. George Thomas, who lived adjacent to the school at Ivy House Farm, at a salary of £18 per annum; note the equal pay! George had been born in the old Toll House on the Tumps (long since demolished), and so, had lived in the shadow of the school for all his life which was to be 93 years, and he always referred to the school as "Lady Hills School", as did all the old folk of that day.

The Taylors had always encouraged thrift, that wonderful word we rarely hear used today, but very relevant in the 1920's and 1930's. So, when a National Schools Savings Association was started, the encouragement to save was well embraced, hence Mr. Bert Taylor's entry: "L.G. Sandford Esq. visited the school this afternoon addressing the scholars on the success of the Schools Savings Association, which had passed £150 in three years".

A few days later, he also wrote: "School closed, an occasional holiday was given by the School Managers in recognition of the growth of the savings," an incentive which was repeated on other occasions. I loved the seams of incentive that seemingly flowed between teacher and pupil, the encouragement to compete and the opportunity to achieve with their daily lessons, in an atmosphere the Taylors had been well versed in providing to this aim so successfully.

"THERE IS ALWAYS A BOOK ON THE SHELF...!"

The last lessons of the week were needlework for the girls and gardening for the boys, which carried a lot of importance in that day, for girls to sew and boys to grow vegetables and, of course, prizes were awarded. The headmaster wrote: "The needlework prizes were given by Mr. L.G. Sandford Esq. and presented by Mrs. Black to the winners of the Upper, Middle and Lower Division, also consolation prizes. At the same time Mrs. Black complimented the girls on the excellent quality of work displayed, which had made her job so time consuming and difficult. The Headteacher proposed a vote of thanks to the Squire and Mrs. Black, which was heartily seconded by the girls."

Likewise of the Gardening Class, prizes were given by Mr. L.G. Sandford Esq., Brigadier General Buston judged the plots and, in his remarks, mentioned that he had, "considerable difficulty in grading them owing to their similarity." When presenting the prizes to the successful boys, he said that he hoped that by giving them in the form of War Savings Subscriptions, it would be a further incentive to thrift.

However, the form of this routine inspection that concentrated thinking of both staff and scholars, was the visitations of HMIS, who seemingly never left a stone unturned. On this occasion they were very pleased with the handwork of the classes, both boys and girls, and commented on what a good variety of articles the children had made from cane and raffia.

They also had inspections from the Local Education Authority (LEA) for physical training and gardening, by Mrs. Davey and Mr. Malthouse. Mr. Quine and Miss Asquith called in to inspect their handiwork and select articles for competition at The West Midland Show, to which Mr. Bert Taylor would avail himself to note the comparisons with other elementary schools.

Other visitations to the school by authorities for inspections of the children were carried out by the Medical Officer, the dentist (who would not give treatment without their parents' consent), the nurse who would check the heads of the children and the most regular visitors were the Vicar and attendance officers.

I love the linkage of time, especially Mr. Bert Taylor's entry in the Log Book that Lilah Thomas had been presented with a first prize in the Upper Division for her needlework. Lilah was the daughter of George Thomas, the school caretaker and lived at Ivy House Farm all her life. She married Cyril Darlington and their son John, after attending Lower Heath School, Whitchurch Grammar School and as an athlete with Birchfield Harriers, became a member of the National High Jumping Team. John was to travel to South America and over Europe, competing to his best height of 5ft. 11ins. and he continued to compete with the seniors until he was 50, his height reduced to 5ft. 9ins. eventually requiring first a new knee and then a new hip.

CHAPTER 54

April, 2019: Miss Parrie's Interview

In 1929 the Shropshire County Library Service opened a book centre at Lower Heath School, receiving the first supply of books on the 7th June, bringing a wonderful asset to both pupils and the local community to access.

In 1932 there was a very sad happening for the school and local community when Squire Sandford tendered his resignation as a school manager, of which he had been chairman for most of his 16 years' service.

Mr. Leslie Gordon Sandford Esq, although totally blind, was regularly seen walking to the school with his white stick. He had devoted much of his time, alongside his wife, to the welfare of the school children and the local community. His unfortunate circumstances, with the demise of Sandford Estates, through no fault of his own, after eight centuries, required his return to London, where he had been a practising lawyer. The school managers' book was always on show at school Open Days, people would comment on the poorness of his signature, however, they were not to know of his blindness and that Mr. Bert Taylor would put the pen in his hand and guide it to the appropriate spot.

Mr. Bert Taylor wrote in conveying the Management's regret on his resignation and thanking him for the active and keen interest he had always taken in the welfare of the school. He also added his own personal thanks for the sympathetic help he had given to him and for the willingness to further any matters in the interests of the scholars.

In 1934 it was recorded in the Manager's book that with the headmasters' tenancy of the school house expiring, it was decided to invite applications for a tenant at a rent of 5s.0d. per week and in due course it was Mr. George Thomas, the school caretaker who moved in. He also had his salary raised from £18 to £20 per annum.

Mr. Bert Taylor having acquired the little croft adjacent to the Tumps, had built himself a very nice residence, also a tennis court, but leaving ample space for the school garden. Earlier it had been the garden for the toll gate family and grazing for a previous headmaster Robert Goffin's pony.

In July 1935, Miss Starkey resigned as Infants teacher and there were 24 applicants for the vacancy, of which a short list of three were considered. After careful consideration by Mrs. Black, Dr. Beckett and carried unanimously, Miss V. Parry was appointed as Certificated Assistant Teacher, having been successful with the interview questions by Mr. Bert Taylor the headmaster, which were as follows:

1. Did you teach infants at all during your two years in college?
2. Had you any course in college with a definite infants and junior bias?
3. You had a P.T. course? Have you attended any P.T. course since leaving college?
4. Broadly what methods would you follow in teaching young children reading?
5. Do you think you could manage a class of 40?
6. Have you found from experience any successful aids to discipline?

"THERE IS ALWAYS A BOOK ON THE SHELF...!"

With Miss Parry having commenced her duties Mr. Bert Taylor wrote: "She seems to be a hardworking teacher and has made a promising start," of course he meant she was fitting into the Taylor mould of teaching with its pleasingly balanced atmosphere, which was underpinned by a steely discipline. Well! Miss Parry was later to be my first teacher, of which I remember fondly and her aid to discipline, if you were naughty, was a rap across the knuckles with the edge of a ruler, to which I was a recipient, an early reminder that to misbehave was to be avoided. Interestingly, Miss Parry's family had had a long association with Fauls Parish. Her great grandfather George Williams being a Surveyor on Hawkstone Estate and the manager of the brickyard at Fauls that made the bricks for the construction of Fauls Church.

The brickyard at Fauls was situated to the rear of what was then The Talbot Inn, conveniently positioned for those hard-working brick makers to partake of a pint. The inn is now Rose Croft and the Williams family lived opposite at Yew Tree Villa, which in that day was a black and white cottage. As for Miss Starkey, the teacher Miss Parry replaced, she had been appointed to a headship in Rugby, a nice way to lose a very good teacher and, "all is well, that ends well."

Yew Tree Villa Williams Family Home (picturing Georges' son)

CHAPTER 55

May, 2019: Absent from School

The 21st December, 1934 arrests my attention with considerable interest, as I peruse through the bygones of Lower Heath School. It being the last entry by the Headmaster Mr. Taylor, in the first school log book – "Closed school for the Christmas Holiday."

The first entry in the first school log book of Lady Hill's (Church of England) School, January 18th, 1872: "Monday commenced school after the usual Christmas holiday (a fortnight) had a very small attendance of children, only 65 present," – by the then headmaster Mr. Goffin.

At this point I am most grateful to the present Headteacher, Mrs. Sadler and her staff, for trawling the nooks and crannies of the school, and providing me with the material to continue my quest of the history of Lower Heath School using log book entries. The first entry in the new log book being on the 7th January, 1935, my starting date had been 26th October 1799, with Industry Hall as the school was first known.

So, the 1930's, like the 1920's and previously, supplied the usual diary of detailed record of the schools' activities in all its aspects. Where local children from 5 to 14 years of age, had the opportunity to take on board the disciplines of a good Elementary Education.

It was also very important to take advantage of all the entertainment available, within the auspices of school, the

"THERE IS ALWAYS A BOOK ON THE SHELF...!"

community and surrounding area. But there were changing entries, apart from the regular calendar which always emphasised singing and sport such as: "School closed, preparation for schools' concerts, which were over two nights and were very well attended and always a big success leaving profit for the sports fund." "School closed, Whitchurch & District School's Festival – holiday. Our Choir of twenty-five sang very well." "School closed for Whitchurch and Wem Carnivals" and entries next day – "very poor attendance," all that trekking having taken its toll.

The prestigious British Legion Sports of the twenties, where Lower Heath youngsters had swept the deck (they still hold the shield) were not mentioned again, and the District School Sports were now held at Wem, where we competed very well, but with not quite the same results. Also, with the departure of the Sandford family, never again were the school to enjoy their annual School Fete in those beautiful grounds of Sandford Hall.

However, Mr. Bert Taylor's entries started to record very special treats for the children – July 4th, 1933: "Church Sunday School excursion to Rhyl". July 5th: "many scholars absent as a result of the excursion yesterday." So, hereafter, whether it was the church or the three Chapels of Darliston, Prees Green or Marchamley Wood, Sunday Schools plus Fauls Church Choir, it was recorded school closed and next day, very poor attendance! Mr. Richard with his Salopian Charabanc coaches (Charabanc *is a large old-fashioned coach with several rows of seats sic Collins Dictionary)*, had brought a new exciting dimension to the youngsters of Lower Heath School with the thrill of the journey and visiting the seaside at Rhyl, most of them for the first time, with all the fun of the fair, no wonder those tired eyelids and legs failed to respond next day with many of them absent.

A Charabanc laden with Prees Villagers for a trip to Llangollen

It was a favourite pastime for lads no longer at school, to gather at Darliston Corner outside Miss Westons shop, often watching the buses from the Midlands come back from Rhyl.

Lads at Darliston Corner

"THERE IS ALWAYS A BOOK ON THE SHELF...!"

There were other times when the headmaster had to record poor attendances for the sad reasons of illness with those winters bringing their mixture of epidemics of influenza, whooping cough, mumps, bronchitis, and measles. At odd times the school was ordered to close for a few days.

Just to mention one troublesome spell recorded in the log book, when the school needed three supply teachers including a headmaster, whose first entry was: "Mr. Lamb (supply) Mr. Bert Taylor – absent through illness" and his second entry: "Owing to an influenza epidemic, attendance very poor." He also recorded spells of very wet weather and snow impairing attendance and as he concluded his duties. When Mr. Bert Taylor returned, his first entry was to report cases of measles to the Medical Officer, of which Miss Active the fourth teacher was to become a victim. The school was ordered to close with only thirty scholars present.

The hoops those children had to go through health wise, and it was good the Schools Medical Officer inspected them on two occasions annually. And the times I heard my mother say, "Kids don't know they are born today."

CHAPTER 56

June, 2019: Building Spree

As a result of Lower Heath School being situated in a very rural area, most of those children's families were involved in agriculture which, with its routine of mostly manual labour, meant their children were well involved in doing parcels of work before and after school hours. However, children of families not involved in agriculture would still spend lots of their time from an early age down on the nearest big farm, it being magic to breathe in and soak up the atmosphere of a working farm, with its complement of animals and busy workers required to tend the husbandry of the stock and land.

I loved to hear Wallace Wilkinson's take on his reminiscing about his early days on the farm adjacent to his home, Coopers of Darliston. Wallace said: "Our mother would say you spend more time on that farm than you do at home." He loved getting involved in all aspects of the goings on, especially the job of taking Shires (horses), by riding on their backs, to be shod by Mr. Abbots, the last blacksmith to work at Sandford. He also added with a smile that Mr. Abbots would always give him a job to do while he waited.

"THERE IS ALWAYS A BOOK ON THE SHELF...!"

The Last Blacksmith at Sandford

The school area comprised of in the tens of big farms and cottages, dozens of smallholdings all adding up to a busy, thriving close knit community all with one thing in common, utmost respect and confidence in the headmaster Bert Taylor and his staff in helping their 130-140 children to achieve their potential, plus they had to sing.

The 1930's saw an increase in building activity locally by Mr. Minshall from Prees, who had built a new house for the headmaster Mr. Bert Taylor. The new build was four blocks of semi-detached council houses at Oakleigh, Lower Heath, and it was said that the same key would open every front door! Also, a new Methodist Chapel at Prees Green was built, which was funded by the congregation, and without debt! The sand for its construction was delivered by horse and cart from the sand hole at Cruckmoor Farm by Richard Chidlow. For the previous chapel, which abutted the A.49, built on land given by Hawkstone Estate in about 1830, Mr. Minshall was paid £10 for its demolition, then he used the bricks on the inside cavity wall of a new house built close by for Mr. Hedge at Sunnyside.

Cruckmoor Lane leading to Cruckmoor Farm Sand Hole

The family of Chesters were well-known locally as bricklayers, their grandfather having been foreman bricklayer on Hawkstone Estate, and there was no better recommendation than that. I well remember the late, eldest grandson Joseph (Chesters) reminiscing, telling me when they started to rebuild Tern Hill in 1935, they were offering bricklayers 1d. an hour above the rate, which in that day was a fortune! And so it was, "make sure the bike tyres are well inflated," and it was Tern Hill bound.

Tern Hill. so named because its slopes abutted the River Tern on its way to the River Severn, had been an airfield during the 1914-18 War. Now home to racing stables and rabbit warrens, it was re-purchased by the Government for the same purpose in 1935.

Of course, that heralded a sad note for our close-knit community, with the possibility of yet another war so soon after the previous conflict; but for two days in May 1935 the school was closed for the Jubilee Celebrations of King George

"THERE IS ALWAYS A BOOK ON THE SHELF...!"

Vth. The school was also closed over two days for the school concerts, where they entertained two large audiences and, after paying expenses there was a balance of £10 14s. 0d.

Miss Heron, (Education Authority, Shirehall), visited the school and inspected the school garden, expressing her satisfaction but was surprised the gardening tools had been in constant use since 1912, the only casualty had been the wheelbarrow, which had been renovated by a local joiner with the Education Committee defraying the cost.

In July 1935, the County Medical Officer ordered the closure of the school because of an outbreak of measles which lingered into August; hence one of the most enjoyable occasions of the school year, the Annual Sports and Prize giving, did not take place.

On a lighter note, an Exhibition and sale of handwork and needlework was a big success, well attended by parents and friends of the school and giving reminders of the beginning of the school as Industry Hall.

CHAPTER 57

July August, 2019: Tern Hill Air Field

As I continue to peruse through the many Lower Heath School Log Book entries, by the Head Teacher Mr. Bert Taylor, I notice he rarely ever mentioned the outside happenings, background, or atmosphere to which his school children were subjected to.

Of this, I am very inclined to avail myself, so as mentioned with the rebuilding of Tern Hill Airfield because of the storm clouds gathering over Europe, Tern Hill was opened to the public for Empire Day on May 23rd 1936, which was also repeated at many other airfields throughout the country. This was an effort to explain to the Country where much of the country's taxes were being spent, and to encourage pride in the country and its armed forces. Tern Hills first opening was a huge success, attracting 1500 people.

The next big celebration was the Coronation of George VI held on 12th May, 1937: "Lower Heath prepares to make merry" with a large Coronation cake baked by Mr. Williams a retired baker, who lived just past the school at The Café, were he and his wife used to serve afternoon teas. There was much excitement for pupils and parishioners alike as the cake was cut at a party held at Lower Heath School.

"THERE IS ALWAYS A BOOK ON THE SHELF...!"

Magnificent Coronation Cake

Tern Hill opening on Empire Day was to be repeated in 1937 and 1938 with ever increasing numbers, and in 1939, 35,000 were to witness the spectacle of aviation at its very best of that day; which had arrived right on our doorstep. The airfield, in full flow, provided a Flying Training School and an Advanced Training Squadron, sharing about 50 aircraft types. Mentioned were Avro Tutors, Hawker Harts, Hawker Audax's, Gloster Gauntlets, Avro Ansons, Hawker Hurricanes, Hawker Fury's, Supermarine Spitfires and Bristol Blenheim's.

The spectators were treated to aerobatic displays, high speed dives, formation flying, parachute descent and anti-aircraft guns in action, defending the station from enemy bombers. A particular thrill was when 9 Blenheim Bombers, in formation at tree top level, arrived over the airfield at exactly 2.00 p.m. hence the song, "Those Daring Young Men in their Flying Machines."

Throughout the afternoon there were lots of other demonstrations, workshops opened, side-shows and, during an interval, the North British Aviation Co. gave a gliding display. The crowd were also entertained by the Royal Air Force Band, with seating and refreshment also provided. The Commanding Officer and his staff had gone to considerable pains to entertain the crowd.

One of the most distinguished pupils to emerge from the training programme was later to become Wing Commander Guy Gibson V.C. (1918-1944), the leader of the Dambusters. It was also said of Guy that one market day in Whitchurch, he flew his aircraft at full throttle up the High Street at chimney pot level, causing a considerable disturbance; hence an immediate ban on low flying aircraft followed.

During these times, Lower Heath School had two concerns in serious need of attention. A new block floor was required in the main body of the school and the small playground badly needed tarmacking. A letter and secondary letters had been sent to the LEA without yet a response. However, one very wet morning, the schools' new Chief Inspector paid a visit and immediately decreed the small playground would be tarmacked – and the LEA would pay 5/6th of the cost.

So, eventually on the 27th February 1939, the headmaster was able to write: "I should like to take this opportunity to thank this Board of School Managers for what proved to be an expensive contribution to the new block floor." Also, the tarmacking of the playground and the partitions around the school had proved a great boon. The amount the School Managers had to contribute to what was a beautiful teak block floor, was not mentioned but there was only £13.0s.6d. left in the school account, hence the requirement of a new flagpole, also required, must not cost more than £2 10s.

"THERE IS ALWAYS A BOOK ON THE SHELF...!"

However, during those years, despite Mr. Bert Taylor not mentioning what happened external to the school, it was mentioned that the Annual Sports, as usual, were a big success and always well attended by parents and friends. The prizes being awarded by Mrs. Foster (nee Miss Gilbert), Mrs. Done, Mrs. F. Davies, and Mrs. T. Morgan. Also, the annual egg collection for the local hospitals by the children in the 4 (classes) numbered 815, 780, 713 and 869 so 3177! and in answer to the Dame Agnes Hunt Appeal, a party of senior scholars and two teachers sang carols for two nights around the Parish with people being unbelievably generous in their donations.

CHAPTER 58

September, 2019; Everton Evacuees

The late 1930's brought a great wind of change for Lower Heath School. The managers, having received notification from the LEA that with the reorganisation of schools, Lower Heath would become a Junior School, with all scholars leaving at the age of 11 and being transferred to Hodnet. Of this, Mr. Bert Taylor did have reservations, specifically about getting all those children, with varying school starting ages, through the necessary classes by 11 years of age; also, about the distances some of the children would have to travel. But for now, it just proved to be the blueprint for the future, because of the atmosphere of the times, with the possibility of war being taken seriously, to which the countries resources were now being channelled. It would be the late 1940's before the split of schools between primary and secondary would come into effect.

Also, at this time there was a wonderful happening in the Parish. The opening of the new Church Hall at Fauls, which had been so generously donated by the Vicar of Fauls, the Rev. Caddick-Adams. Hence, Lower Heath School which since the days of Industry Hall and the passage of 140 years, had been the venue for all social and business activities was now ended. Also, the need of the school managers to complain about the late-night dancing, hilarious activity, and smoking on the premises, would end.

The School Board of Managers received, with sadness, the news that the Rev. H.G. Burton had died at his home in

"THERE IS ALWAYS A BOOK ON THE SHELF...!"

Lincolnshire, having been a school manager and chairman for most of his over 50 years' service, members standing in silence.

On a happier note, Miss Elson, who had been a very much liked teacher for the past 14 years, resigned her duties owing to her forthcoming marriage. During the afternoon, a presentation was made to her from the school managers, staff and scholars consisting of a clock with "Westminster Chimes" and cutlery. The Rev. Caddick-Adams and Headmaster addressed the scholars and the presentation was made by Mrs. Athene Sandford.

On the afternoon of 2nd August 1939, the Schools' Sports were held, bringing the usual measure of excitement with the participation and competition, with many parents and friends in attendance, Mrs. Tom Morgan presenting the prizes. There was also the added flavour for the youngsters when the sports were concluded, with their mothers competing in an egg and spoon race, of which my mother was one of the competitors, and I was now a pupil in Miss Parry's Infants Class.

Mr. Bert Taylor with Teaching Staff (Miss Parry LH side, Miss Active third from LH side, Miss Elson fourth from LH side as you look at the photograph.)

It was all a wonderful prelude for the summer holidays, which they did not know then, was going to be prolonged because at 11.00 a.m. on September 3rd 1939, War was declared and, on the 11th September, Mr. Bert Taylor wrote: "Owing to the outbreak of War, school did not re-assemble until today."

Of course, the consequences were the arrival of the first intake of evacuees from Christ Church C. of E. School, Everton Liverpool, and their teachers.

At first, the double shift system was employed, with Lower Heath children working from 8.30 a.m. – 12.00 noon and Everton School from 12.30 p.m. – 3.45 p.m. After a fortnight, with the return of some evacuees their mothers taking them home, it became possible for half of the school to work full time and eventually, on 20th November, it was possible for all to work full time by merging the remaining evacuees (32) with the local children (123).

On the 27th November, all scholars not having had Measles were excluded from the school until the 11th December – by order of the Medical Officer. This affected about 50 of the children.

The three Everton schoolteachers were the Misses Arrowsmith, Kennedy, and Speakman, all billeted adjacent to the school, which was close to my home and I got to know them all very well. It was obviously a most difficult time for teachers and children away from home and in strange surroundings, but it is fair to say most of those evacuees were to embrace their country cousins and vice-versa, integrating with the local community, creating friendships that were to last a lifetime, and, of course this was repeated in many village and country schools across the land.

"THERE IS ALWAYS A BOOK ON THE SHELF...!"

For most of those town dwelling youngsters, having only been familiar with the surroundings of bricks and mortar, were now transported into a world of green fields, animals, hedgerows, and verges awash with wildflowers and bird song in abundance and it was nothing short of magical.

A Sunday School Class in 1939 including evacuees.
Rogers elder brothers Harry and John West on the
LH side of the back row with John against the arch ...
as you look at the photograph

CHAPTER 59

October, 2019: Bombs Falling

So, as mentioned, the autumn of 1939 for both Lower Heath and Everton Schools now integrated, presented a challenge for both pupils and teachers, getting on with one another, elbow to elbow, with the Everton children quickly blending into school life under our headmaster. In other words, they soon took on board that Mr. Bert Taylor came with an air of authority, conveying an atmosphere that good behaviour was an important key in the continuation of their education, with as little disruption as possible.

However, he also turned another popular key, whereby children were encouraged to do their best, and most importantly, they had got to throw their shoulders back and sing. And with those extra voices, the rendering of an assembly hymn every morning, with its roof raising crescendo and, of course, singing lessons were very much part of his curriculum.

At the turn of the 1940's, on January 19th, "it started to snow, only 50% of scholars in attendance" and on the 26th, "snowing hard, children dismissed at 2.00 p.m.," and eventually, as the weather took its toll, attendance would go down to 15. It was into March before the school and surrounding area would be free from the deep snow drifts and attendance was back to normality; such were the winters of those times. The deep snow-covered landscapes brought an eerie silence to the atmosphere of uncertainty, with War having been declared, but for eight months or so, nothing happened. This period of time would be referred to as the 'Phoney War.'

"THERE IS ALWAYS A BOOK ON THE SHELF...!"

It was late in the summer of 1940 when Tern Hill began to receive a rotation of fighter squadrons, sent for rest periods during the Battle of Britain. Few managed to receive much rest, as they were soon called out on operational sorties in defence of the City of Liverpool. And sadly, as a result, many were shot down over the Irish Sea and in the Welsh mountains.

Safe Return from Bombing Mission WW2

It had been customary for the Bristol Blenheim night fighters returning from a long night to beat up the station before landing; that is, they would fly low over the airfield and buildings. But on the morning of October 16th 1940, what was thought to be a Blenheim doing precisely this, turned out to be a Junkers 88 (a German bomber), which then turned and came in on his bombing run. It released a stick of high explosive incendiary bombs, which smashed through the roof of one of the three massive new hangers, completely demolishing the roof and upper walls and the ten aircraft inside. The Junkers returned on a second run, strafing the mess rooms and domestic quarters, causing considerable casualties, of which no details were known.

The hanger was never rebuilt and became known as the Sunshine Hanger, and it is thought that the Junkers 88 was never intercepted and returned to its base in France.

On November 29th 1940, Mr. Bert Taylor recorded: "Many children absent from school following last night's air raid". He was referring to a stick of four bombs which had fallen, thankfully, in the woods (now pasture) at Lower Heath, which shattered glass in the surrounding properties, including the school. This was to happen in the countryside as a result of German bombers, enroute for Liverpool, encountering extensive flack, causing some of them to turn back and jettison their bombs anywhere.

Next morning, some of the school masters absent children, of which I was one, and lots of other people on bikes, arrived to see the devastation of huge craters, trees strewn like matchsticks and bomb shrapnel, which people gathered for souvenirs. It certainly concentrated our thinking that the unpleasantness of War had arrived on our doorstep. Also, the gratefulness of our community, being able to offer the evacuees shelter and sustenance from the same attacks.

Other Log Book entries at this time: "circularised to parents about action in school, in the event of bombing." They also took delivery of material from the Education Office for the purpose of window blackout and: "The lights went out all over England."

CHAPTER 60

November, 2019: Evacuees Experience

On January 6th 1941, Mr. Bert Taylor's entry read: "School re-opened". During the Christmas holidays there had been the second evacuation of Liverpool children. The infant's class were put-on half-time instruction to accommodate them.

January 20th: "heavy snow falling with bad drifts, 33 out of 176 children present." Children were sent home at 12.00 p.m. owing to increasing drifts, whilst two had been sent home at 11.00 a.m. as they lived further away. On the 15th May the school was to receive the third and final evacuation of Liverpool children, however this time the new Church Hall at Fauls had to be requisitioned to accommodate them and their teachers.

It had all been a wonderful exercise of co-ordination within the community, to meet those youngsters, having arrived at Prees Station late afternoon, in need of sustenance and a room at the Inn. Mrs. Black, who had been one of the School Managers, and Doctor Franklyn, the local doctor, led the team of helpers, especially those few people of that day who possessed motor cars to transport the children and to knock on doors to find them a home and a haven away from the blitz of Liverpool.

I love the story that Jimmy, and Ronnie Henderson arrived on the doorstep of No. 2 Darliston, weary, stressed, one stale bun between them, carrying their gasmasks and their ration books. Mrs. Wilkinson assessed their requirements and dispatched her son Wallace on the Salopian Bus to Whitchurch to purchase all the necessary little luxuries to make those two youngsters welcome and as comfortable as possible. That act of kindness, forming a bond which was to last with the Christmas card and the odd drop-in for over half a century, plus my memory which reminds me Jimmy Henderson was a very good footballer.

On 29th May, 1942, it became possible to transfer the remainder of the evacuees from Fauls Hall back to the school, due to the reduction in numbers by children reaching the age of 14, together with other evacuee returnees to Liverpool.

In January 1995, the children of Lower Heath did a project on the 1939-45 War, (coordinated by Sam, James, Eve, and Chris), advertising in the Liverpool Echo for help from ex-evacuees to share their experiences of being evacuated to the parish. They were delighted with the response, receiving twenty letters with stories about how they left home for strange places, clutching their teddy-bears to escape the cruel consequences of Hitler's bombs. The one theme that came to the fore in answer to the advert was surprise and delight that they were doing a project on part of the history of the War they thought had been badly neglected.

With the evolution of time, I can pin-point several of those letters with reference to Lower Heath School but, in general, they "well grasp" the atmosphere of those troubled times and their silver linings with their reminiscences. So, visiting their memories of fifty years past, the content of which permits me to relate the cruel necessity that began the plight of the evacuees: "I will never forget that morning, coming out of the air raid shelter, seeing our church and school (Everton) burning, everyone crying, even the Vicar, then walking home seeing bombed and burning houses, people being brought out dead, children dead, the bombing going on, day in and day out."

"THERE IS ALWAYS A BOOK ON THE SHELF...!"

"When the sirens went, you grabbed your tin hat, gas mask and ran to an underground shelter. A lot of people took a chance and stayed in their houses, some were lucky and some not so lucky, I still shiver when I hear a siren." And in a similar vein: "I was evacuated to North Shropshire following the May Blitz of 1941, when a large proportion of the city was destroyed, leaving many families homeless, my own included. Some of those bombs, meant for the docks, hit a maternity home killing mothers and their babies; my mother said enough was enough and decided to evacuate us. We were marched to the Railway Station, clutching our gas masks, ration books, some food – including a tin of corned beef, amidst a flood of tears heading for the unknown."

But on a far more cheerful note, that unknown was to become for the vast majority, as relayed in their own words: "A haven of joy and kindness" with lots of stories as mentioned of No. 2 Darliston.

Rev. Caddick Adams Whitsunday Sunday School (1942)
Fauls Green Church (Roger is second from RH side
second row from back and his sister Cynthia
is second one from RH side front row)

CHAPTER 61

December, 2019/January, 2020: The Benefits of Drinking Milk

For Lower Heath School and, of course, for lots of country schools, evacuees were to become an integral part of daily life, their stay lasting from three to five years. There were also, as recorded by the headmaster, about ten or a dozen children referred to as private evacuees. These were children with family connections locally, coming from Liverpool, Manchester, and London, and the school register recording a total of 211 at its highest.

It all added up to a very busy atmosphere, and one detects the intensity of the times through the increased log book entries, chronicling the day-to-day flow of the school business.

The visitations of the Local Authority, School and Medical officials were noticeably more prominent. HMIS, instead of their annual full day at the school, would now drop in several times a year to examine a particular class or teacher for about an hour. The children were subjected to medical inspections but I notice now parents' consent was required for their immunisation against Diphtheria and for dental treatment. This meant the distribution of forms, collection and forwarding to the Medical Officer and on one occasion Mr. Bert Taylor recorded the highest consent for dental treatment was 75%. This treatment was now taking four days, for which there was a charge which was collected by Mr. Bert Taylor for the education accountant. Medical inspections were over three days, but the most regular visitor was the Nurse for head lice inspections, several times a year.

Also, at this time the children became involved in helping with the War effort in various ways by collecting sacks of bones, aluminium articles, and waste paper. There was a National Savings Week for "Wings for Victory" of which the school was a centre, which realised £2176 11s. with £130 of contributions invested by the scholars.

A lady visiting gave the children a talk on the benefits of drinking milk and the headmaster, after negotiations with the Education Office and parents, enabled the introduction of the school milk scheme, giving the children the opportunity to have a beaker of milk every morning. The milk was supplied by Mr. Gollins of Fauls Farm.

The intensity of school officialdom was such, I will use Mr. Bert Taylors own words to describe it, not recorded in the Log Book but, scribbled at the bottom of a page in a note book: "Rightly or wrongly, I think all Head teachers take the view, that the powers that be now regard these extraneous duties as of more importance than the real school work" ... listing all those non actual educational activities.

However, there was a War on, and all hands-on deck were important. Schools throughout the country being given three weeks holiday in September to help on the farms with the potato harvest. Mr. Bert Taylor did not have this out of school activity on his list, he probably thought, as indeed we all did, this was a brilliant learning curve to have access to a big dairy farm, an opportunity for work experience, and best of all we got paid.

So, to re-visit my early memories of potato picking, pooled with those of the Liverpool evacuees in their reminiscing letters, potato picking being lodged very highly. One lady wrote: "My memories are vague, but we lived with a family named Heath – who were very good to us – by a big lake, the Schoolmaster was Mr. Bert Taylor, we also went to Fauls Sunday School. One thing we loved doing was crossing the road to the farm and watching the cheese being made." This one was easy to identify, – Noden's Farm at Sandford, and it was where I, together with a mixture of locals and evacuees, spent two holidays harvesting potatoes. We were all twelve and over, and our working hours were the same as schooling, 9.00 a.m. to 12 noon and 1.00 p.m. to 3.00 p.m., and we were well informed of the time schedule by the Sandford Hall clock that struck the hour and chimed the quarters, even so, they were to be long back aching days.

Noden's Farm Sandford

One lady evacuee wrote: "Working in conjunction with the Farm personnel and especially those beautiful Shire horses, one did not seem to mind the odd potato that flew through the air, targeting our up-turned buttocks, or the worms dropped down our wellington tops."

The two Shires that hauled the potato digger were always changed at dinner time and one afternoon a young Shire, being broken in, was introduced with an older Shire, which led to a rivetingly memorable occasion. His tantrums of rearing and expressing his dislike for the whole procedure was more than equally matched by the horsemanship and skill of his handler. Needless to say, that horse was to be avoided, whilst the other Shires were contented to carry several youngsters on their backs on the trek to and from the potato field.

The highlight of the days' work was when we all queued up and Mr. Noden paid us with a half-crown (worth 12.5 pence) and a florin (worth 10 pence today). Somehow our aching backs and legs and the long walk home did not seem too bad, also, I bet Mr. Bert Taylor thought it was a valuable contribution to our education.

CHAPTER 62

February, 2020: Salute the Soldiers Week

Apart from the sad circumstances resulting in the plight of the evacuees and their integration into our local school and community at Lower Heath, it was to prove a big success. All through the initial difficulties of packed classrooms and playground, with the progress of time, the evacuees on reaching the age of fourteen years, then returned to Liverpool. Also now, with the fluctuations of the War, the sad and upsetting reports of the destruction of Liverpool and the fires that could be seen from the various high ground in Shropshire, were now thankfully in the past.

By now, we were being treated to a different aspect of the War taking place immediately above our playground, which was right under the circuit of the Whitley Bomber aircraft, training the aircrews from the recently completed airfield at Prees Heath. This was referred to as circuit and bumps and was to go on 24 hours a day for about 12 months. These being replaced by Stirling Bombers or towing gliders, now training ready for the Normandy landings, as part of the D-Day planning for Operation Overlord (sic. IWM.org.uk).

"THERE IS ALWAYS A BOOK ON THE SHELF...!"

Returning to Prees Heath in a Snow Blizzard after Laying Mines in the North Sea (Photo given to dad by a good friend Mr. Tyrer who is one of the airmen in the picture)

So, all that activity above became part of our early lives but hardly noticed, as the serious business of the playground football games, into which every bit of effort, energy, skills, and enthusiasm were brought to bear. The teams were changed every day, so the rough and tumble, the odd rattling of shins were all dispensed in a good-natured atmosphere and soon brought to a close by Mr. Bert Taylor's whistle; and tomorrow was another day.

Another out of classroom activity which arrested a considerable amount of everyone's attention, especially the evacuee boys, who most of them for the first time were now introduced into the wonderful world of growing vegetables.

However, there were not enough plots in Mr. Bert Taylor's Garden to cater for the numbers, so, on the 9th March 1942, he wrote in the Log Book: "Commenced to fence and cultivate area at the bottom of the big playground". It was all in the atmosphere of the times, when the country was being encouraged, by the slogan "Dig for Victory" and to produce as much food as possible.

Miss Heron, the LEA garden visitor, expressed her satisfaction at the quality of the garden plots. She also brought tools and an extra wheelbarrow and it was noticed for the first time, that she brought artificial manure! I suppose that was to complement the horse and cart load of farmyard manure delivered by Mr. Davies of School Farm and tipped up in the gateway or the corner of his field which abutted the school garden.

Hence, Mr. Bert Taylor was able to write, underlining the satisfaction of the garden inspector and I would think also his own: "Our largest potato weighed 2lbs. 10 oz. and a Liverpool boy returning home, on becoming 14 years of age, took with him our largest garden swede of 20lbs."

It was a sad occasion for the school and local community when the Headmaster, Mr. Bert Taylor, recorded the death of his father Mr. Robert Taylor, who had been the Headmaster of Lower Heath School from 1875-1919.

On a happier note, on the 23rd December, 1943 a presentation of cutlery from scholars, teachers and managers was made to Miss Gilbert, on the occasion of her forthcoming marriage. Miss Gilbert had commenced her duties as teacher on the 31st January, 1940.

"THERE IS ALWAYS A BOOK ON THE SHELF...!"

On 14th December 1943, Mr. Campbell, an evacuated Headteacher from Wem, called to say the people of Liverpool were sending a Christmas grant for the evacuees. Also, a Mr. Lawrie visited the school one afternoon to speak about a "Book Drive" fortnight, to which the children were to respond by collecting a total of 2053 books.

For "Salute the Soldiers Week" (1944) the children seemingly had done a fantastic job of the advertisement placards outside the school, which was used as a selling centre by The Schools Savings Association, and realised the sum of £4557 2s.0d for the civil sponsorship of army equipment. During that week, Mr. Rolleston-Hayward, the Chief School's Inspector visited and Mr. Bert Taylor made a note, not in the Logbook but in his notebook: "that he would point out the placard display and remind him that there are many aspects of education in schools today."

CHAPTER 63

March, 2020: Yellow Balls of Fluff

I suppose it is fair to say with my generation, most of our schooling was experienced within the atmosphere of wartime, with all its restrictions, rationing, the displacement of our Liverpool cousins who arrived amongst us, which all added up to a very rewarding experience. As mentioned previously, with all the aerial activity over our playground, the final episode of the Stirling bombers with their gliders in training, prior to the Normandy Landings, which was to herald the final stages of the 1939-45 War.

Incidentally, there had been 60 fully trained crews ready at Prees Heath, but they were not used in the Normandy Landings, however three weeks later they were all involved at Arnhem, with its tragic consequences. (At Arnhem, "1,485 British and Polish airborne troops were killed or died of wounds and, 6,525 more became prisoners of war ... As an indicator of the courage displayed by the British forces, five Victoria Crosses were awarded – four of them posthumously." IWM.org.uk.)

As Mr. Bert Taylor would mention, there were many aspects of education to do with schooling and the integration of Liverpool and local youngsters was most important. Bonding and friendships were formed which brought bits of magic to everyday life.

I know of only one photograph taken of Lower Heath school children during the War, other than Sunday School groups and, being on them I remember them being taken very well. One afternoon on leaving school, a lady appeared and was determined to photograph as many children as possible who were willing, which was to be 44, and luckily, I have got one in front of me to refresh my memories of those times and acquaintances.

Photograph of Lower Heath School Kids Taken During the War (Roger is the 4th boy from the left on the backrow and his sister Cynthia is second child from RH side bottom row)

Looking at the photograph with fond memories, I notice the Lipson twins and McMullins twins (second and third in from the LH side second row from front) and their older sister (same row third one in from RH side), each in a tartan dress.

The two Lipson girls, Stella and Rosie, evacuees who with our local contingent, were very much part of our school run and classroom for the span of their enforced stay amongst us. The Lipson girls were very noticeable, with masses of red hair, and were billeted with Mr. & Mrs. Gilbert who were smallholders living at the Stone House, Lower Heath and having no children of their own, treated those two girls as their own. It was a similar story with the McMullen girls, who were billeted with Mr. & Mrs. Edge at Sunnyside, who, being a bit elderly, and with no children of their own, extended every kindness to make those girls, who always seemed to appear in tartan dress, as comfortable as possible.

The Stone House on the Lower Heath Straight

There is also a photograph of the Sunday School group (found in Chapter 66) with 50 children on it, taken at Faul's Church, with its contingent of evacuees, of which one of them, Enid Cumerlidge, was to respond to the advert School placed in the Liverpool Echo. Enid, who was a bit younger than me, would relate her experiences as an evacuee. She had read the advert with considerable interest and for the first time started to record her experiences so indelibly imprinted in her memory, of the destruction of her home and a train journey into the unknown, not minding where she went but hoped there would be another little girl she could play with. Ford Farm, Darliston was to be her destination, the home of Mr. & Mrs. Hull and

"THERE IS ALWAYS A BOOK ON THE SHELF...!"

their family of three older boys and a younger girl. Her initial hopes pleasantly answered and they are standing side by side on our Sunday School photograph.

Enid had been evacuated from Arnot Street Primary School, Walton, Liverpool, they were to be the last arrivals and with no room at the school, she, and their teachers, as she described it, were accommodated in a "wooden hut" at a place called Fauls for their lessons. However, after about six months, room became available at the school, to which she now walked with the family and joined by several of her Liverpool friends who were staying at houses on the way.

I had a brilliant day, fulfilling my desire of many years, to visit the Eisteddfod at Llangollen, returning home (although tired) with a wonderful feeling of satisfaction. I was then informed that the two Lipson girls had visited the Stone House and walked our school run, and I was very sad now. I would have loved to have done that with them again, 70 odd years on! Rosie was my age, Stella older, she was a bit bossy but I liked her.

Would she have remembered consoling me having lost one of my bantam hens to the fox?

Would she have remembered the rejoicing when my bantam returned three weeks later, trailing twelve little yellow balls of fluff? .... sadly, those questions were left hanging in the air!

CHAPTER 64

September, 2020 (Published 4 months later, due to Covid-19): Eating Well

The history of Lower Heath School, in relationship to the Liverpool evacuees is well documented by the hand of the headmaster and still within the grasp of memories that in general refer to the excitement and pleasure that shone through those unfortunate circumstances. So, as one who was also part of that experience, it is with considerable pleasure I can now meander further through those written memories of the evacuees, which brought a lovely balance of respect and appreciation between town and country cousins.

Of course, all evacuees missed their families and longed to be back at home; but children soon settle down aided with visitations by parents, usually mothers, some by train and others by bus, monthly on a Sunday.

One of the most important things those youngsters were to latch onto, due to rationing and only being used to small amounts of food... they were amazed at what the countryside had to offer. One wrote of being delighted to have a big duck egg for breakfast every morning and another had never seen so much butter. They were to enquire: "Don't you have rationing in the country?" Yes, we did.... but within a farming area awash with smallholders and their complement of farmyard animals, poultry, geese, ducks plus the contributions from the wildlife of pheasant and rabbit, this ensured the pot and plate were well provisioned.

"THERE IS ALWAYS A BOOK ON THE SHELF...!"

The contribution of Prees and Fauls evacuees, with their reminiscing letters with comments like: "Those four to five years were the best of my life;" ... people and times remembered with much affection and a general thinking that their lot was a part of War History that had been neglected. The youngsters, who were never made to feel outsiders, soon latched on to the magic of the countryside and the codes of conduct that came with it... one must not leave gates open and you do not trample hayfields.

John Paul, one of the Prees evacuees who responded to the Liverpool Echo advert 50 years after the end of World War II, brought so much clarity, details, and joy of being part of the Village during those times. John had been taken in by Mr. & Mrs. Gibbons of Brades Cottages and his sister Elsie by Mr. & Mrs. Williams, where one water tap served all the cottages, and oil lamps were used for lighting. It became John Paul's job to fetch the water when needed. There was a traditional brick toilet situated at the bottom of the garden, which had to be emptied every so often. He writes: "this had its rewards being recycled to ensure the vegetables and flowers, pinks and carnations produced enormous blooms which were sold at Market Drayton Market."

Ducks were also kept for eggs and the table at Christmas. These were let out onto the stream which ran at the bottom of the garden to forage, and Mrs. Gibbons made jam in a big brass cooking pot on the open fire, plus rabbit stew was often on the menu ... yes! we lived so well.

Prees School was on the top of the hill by the church and Mr. Unwin, the schoolmaster at Prees, used to get the children to dig and work in his garden, which we all enjoyed. John Paul also sang in the church choir and if you did not sing, you were made to pump the organ and on one occasion, as a treat, we were taken to the pictures at Shrewsbury to see Robin Hood with Errol Flynn in it. At holiday time John Paul loved going with Mr. Gibbons, who worked for a nursery, taking the produce by horse and cart to Whitchurch Friday Market, also visiting Prees Heath swimming baths and, at eleven years old, John Paul went to Wem Grammar School, travelling in an old ramshackle bus. John Paul ended his letter to Sam, James, Eve, and Chris of Lower Heath School: "Trusting this letter will be of some help for your project."

I am sure they were thrilled to bits with it, I certainly was, because as one of the several letters from Prees evacuees it captured the general flavour and atmosphere of those times, although John Paul did not mention the bombing of Liverpool from which they all sort solace.

CHAPTER 65

October, 2020: Wild Flowers

The School Log Book, with its day-to-day jottings, permits one to meander into the general affairs of the school's business, visitations, with always an emphasis on absenteeism, especially teachers, but rarely any mention of classroom activity or lessons. I remember very well my first attendance in the infant's class, with the top classes through an adjacent door, and the rendering of the morning hymn with its roof raising volume to such a degree I burst into tears. Those were the only tears I shed during my nine years stay at Lower Heath School and eventually being part of hymn singing and singing lessons every week – so much part of the Taylor's curriculum – one had to throw one's shoulders back and sing, justice had to be done to the Ash Grove, The Minstrel Boy to the War has Gone, The Skye Boat Song, Shenandoah, and Old Father Thames; tunes that are forever with me.

Being a Church of England School, with regular visits from the Vicar, I notice that the Trust Deed of the school states: "the Chairman of the School Managers was responsible for the supervision of religious instruction given in the school." So, our regular visitations by the Vicar, with lessons about the Holy Lands of Palestine, involving the hub of the surrounding countries, he always arrested our attentions with his detail, background, rise and fall of Empires, so giving us all a good awareness of those happenings.

There was always a touch of excitement when new lessons were introduced and especially when we went up a class but, there was one lesson that really captured our attention and harnessed our enthusiasm; Nature Study Lessons. Miss Annie Active, our teacher, had arrived at Lower Heath School in 1926 at the age of 18 on her bike and, after her successful interview, was to stay for nearly 40 years. Having been born in the countryside, in the days when the hedgerows and verges were awash with wildflowers, she had developed a passion for the countryside bringing it into our Nature Study lessons. The school inspectors report of that day' encouraged the subject of Nature Study, so much so that our regular drawing lessons and Miss Active's bent for the former, meant drawing and painting wild flowers became a must, ... and such an enjoyable lesson.

Occasionally she would take us on nature study walks. Very disciplined, walking two by two, usually over the stile, through Lady Hill's Coach Drive, over the road and up Yew Tree Lane, which was always awash with wild flowers. There were frequent stops to draw our attention to a particular flower, explaining its petals, leaves, shape, veins, and colours. Detail as nature had produced it was vital. Some youngsters used to refer to her as 'Naggy Annie,' but that was only because she demanded the utmost attention and concentration, as in the Taylor regime style, which was for our own benefit

To perpetuate this interest, Miss Active issued a challenge to her class, of how many species of wild flowers could we collect in a given period. The child being first with a particular flower on Monday mornings got the point. Miss Active wrote: "I have a book of wild flowers collected in 1939/40, drawn by myself and painted by the child bringing the specimen," ... paper and paint were scarce commodities then!

"THERE IS ALWAYS A BOOK ON THE SHELF...!"

Annie Actives Sketch

Annie Actives Sketch

The children from Liverpool took part and they did very well. These paintings were done on strips of paper, six on each strip and put on show, the final total being 341, and used as a challenge for future classes. One of which, in 1952, added 23 more to the list. On her retirement, they were bound into a book and given to her as a present; I have the book in front of me now. It appears children who had the greatest distance to travel to school did better, and the most successful collector, by a considerable margin, was to be a friend of mine, Tommy Speed, and the book prize they gave him was to be highly treasured by him for the rest of his life.

Those nature lessons of Miss Active, on the treasures of hedgerows, verges, and countryside, were to be forever with me and I have had considerable pleasure in laying wild flowers on her grave many times; to which she chose four of her Lower Heath pupils, including me, to be her bearers and convey her there.

Another memory of our Yew Tree Lane walks, with its wide verges, was that it was a regular stopping place for the Romany Gypsies, with their gaily coloured homes on wheels, tethered Piebald ponies, several Lurcher dogs, pots simmering over a wood burning fire and the washing spread over the hedgerows drying. The men and women, apart from living off the land, did valuable work on local farms at harvest time, especially with the harvesting of mangolds and swedes, a big part of cattle feed in that day.

This colourful itinerant way of life pursued for centuries, like so many of the wild flowers we once enthusiastically collected from the verges and hedgerows of the Parish, now just a part of the past.

CHAPTER 66

November, 2020: "Life on the Farm"

On the 5th October 1943, Miss Arrowsmith, the last of the four Liverpool teachers was recalled, heralding the end of the evacuee stay at Lower Heath School, which had begun in September 1939, at the outbreak of the 1939-45 War. Miss Arrowsmith had arrived with the first batch of evacuees and Mr. Bert Taylor the headmaster wrote that, "she had been a great help throughout those difficult times and often took charge of his class when other duties took him away." She had been well liked and fitted the Taylor mould of teaching, dispensing her duties with firmness in a kindly way, rarely ever raising her voice, hence Mr. Bert Taylor's high praise of her.

By now, most of the evacuees (apart from five), had returned to Liverpool including Enid Cumerlidge, who was to visit the school fifty years later in answer to the school project and wrote a well detailed, and interesting account of her experiences of which I will visit again here.

"I remember with much affection life 'on the farm' with Mr. & Mrs. Hull and family at Ford Farm, Darliston, helping to fetch the cows up for milking and in the dairy, feeding the hens and collecting eggs, learning to ride my bicycle and my most cherished memory was riding to meet my parents off the train, who were always invited to the farm at Christmas time. I walked to school in clogs and up the bank to Sunday School in my best shoes, but being a little girl from the city I did not like clogs, so Mrs. Hull bought me shoes with rubber over the wood strap fastenings instead of laces. I also went to the

Methodist Chapel Anniversary which was the annual event for the village." I too remember walking to school in clogs and best shoes on a Sunday.

Enid also loved the summer holidays and being taken by Mr. & Mrs. Hull, on Wednesdays, to Market Drayton and the hustle and bustle of the market, caring for the bantams she was given, collecting wild flowers, particularly cowslips, and water cress. Chasing rabbits at harvest time and helping to gather fruit from the large orchard, apples, plums and especially damsons. Skating, or rather sliding on ice in the wintertime. Enid's letter was to echo the general feeling of the evacuee's contentment of their enforced stay with us and I will again use her words to be the final ones on this subject.

"I cannot complete these memories without acknowledging a debt of gratitude to Mr. & Mrs. Hull and family and all the other families in the area who so willingly accepted strangers into their homes during a period of history which I trust will never, ever again be repeated."

That awful bombing of Liverpool, responsible for the distortion of so many people's lives, including the very sad bereavement for the Trevor family of Prees, bringing shock and sadness to the Village in which he was born and grew up in. I have in front of me detail of his bravery and a scrolling that commemorates him.

> "Constable Alan Trevor, Liverpool City Police Force,
> held in honour as one who served King and Country
> in the World War of 1939-1945 and gave his life
> to save mankind from tyranny.
> May his sacrifice help to bring the peace and
> freedom for which he died."

"THERE IS ALWAYS A BOOK ON THE SHELF...!"

Alan had been captain of the tower bell ringers at Prees Church.

1944 was to be an eventful year for the school staff. Two of the teachers, Miss Active and Miss Gilbert, were married with presentations to them both on behalf of scholars, staff, and management. Mr. George Thomas resigned as school caretaker, at the age of 73, and he received a letter from the management committee expressing their thanks for his work as caretaker over the past 17 years. Of the seven new applicants for the job, Mr. Percy Davies of Lower Heath was selected. Percy, who was the local postman, and his mother had been the last surviving tenant of Hawkstone Estate. He had also just married Miss Annie Active.

For Miss Active, who already lived on the school premises, it entailed her moving into the part which had been the school master's house, now as the wife of the new caretaker, becoming Mrs. Davies. The school house had been visited previously by the Managers, who had ordered the various alterations and repairs including a new roof and cooking range, the kitchen floor boards, guttering, drainage to be improved and it was agreed Mr. George Ward should undertake the work, which was all approved, and his account of £98 1s. 0d. should be paid.

Mr. Davies, who did not enjoy the best of health, having been gassed in the 1914/18 War, thought the remuneration for the job of 18s.0d, per week was scant reward for such a consuming job and wrote to the school managers, suggesting it should be increased. The school managers were unanimous and applied to the LEA, who also agreed and Mr. Davies' salary was raised to 20s. 0d. per week.

Fauls Green Church Sunday School 1944 Whitsunday, with Sunday School teachers Mrs. Dean and Mrs. Hocknell (Looking at the photograph, Roger is second in from LH side back row, with Johhny Benbow is on the LH side and Brian Morris on the RH side)

CHAPTER 67

December, 2020/January, 2021: Links to Australia

Mr. Bert Taylor's entries in the School Log Book for the 8th and 9th of May 1945, were so brief: "School closed VE Day" but, he also wrote for the 8th May, that Janet Scarr had gained admission to a Secondary School in Essex. It was all heralding, thankfully, the end of the War in Europe, also Janet – who was the same age as me at 13, – represented the last of the evacuees to leave Lower Heath School. Janet had been a private evacuee, having spent the War years with relatives at Sandford.

In fact, 1945 was to be a very pivotal year for the school, with Mr. Bert Taylor recording that the school attendance, at 86, was the least for twenty-six years. Lower Heath School was now organised into three groups, Class I years 11, 12, 13, Class II years 8,9,10, Class III years 5,6,7, (ages are approximate only). Mr. Bert Taylor wrote: "This meant with supervision during the mid-day break, teachers were to have less time for lunchbreaks."

It must have been a sad meeting of the School Managers when the Chairman referred to the loss the Committee had sustained through the deaths of their late Chairman the Rev. Caddick-Adams and Dr. Beckett. Both had served on the Board of Management for long periods and were always ready to help him in any way they possible could. The Committee stood in silent tribute and the Headteacher was requested to write to Mrs. Beckett, expressing their sympathy.

The Rev. Caddick-Adams M.A. was a regular visitor on Monday mornings to check the school register, also between 40 and 50 of us attended his Sunday School at Fauls. He was a bachelor, very tall, very serious and a kindly Vicar who had spent his time as a Curate in Australia, where he told us it took him three months to go around his Parish on horseback. At Fauls, as mentioned previously, he was regularly seen around his Parish on a sit-up and beg bicycle with his little dog Tojo, named after the Prime Minister of Japan, chasing after him. He demanded, deserved, and got our utmost respect.

On several occasions Miss Parry had been loaned to Hodnet School, and eventually the LEA moved her permanently to Tilstock School. So, Miss Parry, who had been my first teacher, terminated her duties as certificated assistant teacher on 30th November 1945, having completed ten years at Lower Heath School. She had been a very good teacher, in the Taylor mould: "you must get on with your work and don't chatter."

Miss Violet Parry had originally been chosen for the job out of twenty-four applicants. She came from Tilstock, but her family roots had been at Fauls, whereby her great grandfather, George Williams, was land agent on Hawkstone Estate. He was also Manager of Lord Hill's Brickyard at Fauls, from where the 88,000 bricks had been made for the building of Fauls Church and many other buildings in the Parish. George lived at Yew Tree Cottage, Fauls and had two sons. His first son George, Miss Parry's grandfather, was a carpenter and his second son Robert was a draper and had run his own business in Liverpool.

Robert married a daughter of one of Everton Football Club's Directors and, on his retirement, came back to Fauls to Yew Tree Cottage. Both boys were pupils of Lady Hill's School, Lower Heath and would reminisce about summer evenings visiting the Talbot Inn opposite Rose Croft, seeing the farm hands and brickyard workers (the brick works were at the rear of Rose Cottage) at the tables and chairs on the lawn with their flagons of ale. On his return, Robert proceeded to apply gable windows and bays, pebble-dash, and arches to their Tudor black and white Yew Tree Cottage; he also grew some of the best vegetables in the district.

The year (1945) had begun with January's usual contribution of a complete white-out, snow several feet deep, devastating attendance of both staff and pupils. Also, the school had experienced a severe gale, dislodging roofing slates and a pane of glass in the west window was blown in, falling on several children. Fortunately, no-one was hurt.

However, the children were to enjoy a ray of sunshine as Mrs. Whitcombe, from a sheep station in Victoria, Australia arrived at the school and distributed sweets and little treats to the scholars. She was on holiday visiting her sister, Mrs. Britton, where two of the Liverpool evacuee teachers, Miss Arrowsmith and Miss Kennedy had stayed.

CHAPTER 68

February, 2021: Miss Gilbert

On the 30th April 1946, Mrs. Foster (nee Miss Gilbert) resigned as an assistant teacher at Lower Heath School. She had been one of my three lady teachers. and it also heralded the end of my days and elementary education at Lower Heath. So, I well remember her as she was then, Miss Gilbert, starting at the school and contributing to the collection for her wedding present and Mr. Bert Taylor, Headmaster, saying a few words about her. Her first job had been at Hodnet School and he said he remembered this young lady cycling past his gate every morning, in all weathers, spot on time, and when she applied for the vacancy at Lower Heath, being one of three, she got it!

Miss Gilbert had lived on a small holding at Prees Wood, where her father had been a very familiar figure around the Village of Prees, delivering milk in his pony and trap which he would ladle into the containers placed on door steps. On April 1st 1946, Mrs. Fearnall of Manor House Lane was appointed unanimously by the School Managers, following the resignation of Mrs. Foster.

To say I enjoyed every minute of my years at Lower Heath School would be a gross understatement and it still gives me considerable pleasure to meander through the history of the school and to revisit memories of my time there. But, as mentioned, apart from my first day at school, when the rendering of the morning hymn was so loud I burst into tears; that was the beginning for me of what most people would say were the best days of our lives.

"THERE IS ALWAYS A BOOK ON THE SHELF...!"

My excitement of learning to read and write, and with being a Church of England School, the day always began with scripture lessons. Also acquiring friends and most importantly, getting on with your work, do not chatter, all very much underlined by my mother, and, "you must not be late home from school Roger!" On reflection, with the mixture of scripture and history lessons concentrated on the biblical and surrounding lands within the five seas, all presented in such a way captured our interest. Hence, we progressed through the centuries as Greeks, Egyptians, Romans, Syrians, Persians, Carthaginians et al, in their turn, building empires at the expense of one another. In so doing, achieving whatever opulence of that day in their culture, architecture, art, mathematics, astronomy but, by now fifty of their beautiful cities mostly buried beneath the ground.

I remember when a new subject or lesson was introduced, whether fractions or decimals, there was always a ripple of excitement and expectation, especially when we went up a class. I think it was a wonderful atmosphere with the giving and receiving of knowledge, plus the competitive element when we were given marks out of ten for our efforts to take it all on board and very importantly, one's workings in the margin of how our answers were arrived at. Having progressed through the classes, being taught by our three local teachers and at times by teachers from Liverpool, it was now my turn to go through classes 5, 6, and 7 with Mr. Bert Taylor the Headmaster.

That concentrated my thinking; 'The Boss,' always immaculately dressed in a suit, over 6ft. tall, was a very imposing figure and we held him with the utmost respect, that being the first basic we took on board, which was lesson number one. However, it was to be a concentration that never wavered. Now, apart from routine subjects, we were introduced to sport, singing and gardening (sewing for the girls). It was all served up in an atmosphere that seemingly came with a natural built-in motivation, that, "he wanted you to do well" or whatever measure one could ascribe to.

With singing, we had to raise the roof, and with poetry we had to write the verses out, take them home, then memorise them, and then at random the next day he would invite anyone of us to stand in front of the class and recite those lines. I will forever remember Ena Mapp in her blue frock and blonde hair, beautifully reciting 'Leisure,' delivered without hesitation or prompting, and the boss just smiling; yes, the bar was certainly nudged into position for the rest of us to trail.

English lessons were another challenging time, a given subject... discussions... he encouraged questions... then write about it for me... in your own words. His teaching was so helpful, plus he would often mention such and such a book, which was available for anyone who wanted to further their knowledge on any subject. It was a pleasure to have been one of his pupils.

CHAPTER 69

March, 2021: Foxes and Hounds

To reminisce, recalling memories and experiences of one's school days, for me is a total pleasure, it is a pity those seasons came and went so quickly. For my schooling, which spanned the War years of 1939-45, when all of today's modern facilities, piped water, flushing toilets, electricity, canteens, school meals and taxis were very much still in the future, but nothing deterred one's opportunity to generate enthusiasm for what we had.

So memorable were those nasty cold, wet, snowy winters, but we knew whatever the weather on our journeys to school, it was always best to be early and we would be greeted by the warmth of those massive coke burning stoves. These would have been lit by the caretaker at 6 o'clock in the morning and those substantial railing guards on three sides were ideal for, which was the rule, any wet clothing to be dried and shoes were placed around its base.

Also, and most importantly, was the toasting forks and the stove, which turned our cheese, spam, jam butties into hot meals in seconds, all accomplished within a very humorous atmosphere. However, we were all very aware of those difficult times with the B.B.C. News broadcasts of Alvar Lidell** about the fluctuations of our forces in North Africa, the names of our various generals and places mentioned during the conflict were all followed on the map and discussed.

Yes, those winters did provide us with that extra challenge. But summers were a joy, with the balance of both classroom and playground, also sitting in circles on the grass in our various groups with our midday sandwiches and forever involved in dialogue.

Then playtime, mostly always football, but on odd occasions it was decided, by the two senior boys, that we would play 'Fox and Hounds.' The four corners of the playground being marked out as the dens, and the nominated fox who, after the count of ten, had to break cover. This gave vent to the sprinters, rugby tacklers all exercised with extreme competitiveness, making it riveting viewing for everyone, including the girls. Of course, whoever was judged to have brought the fox down, then became the fox, all abruptly ended by Mr. Bert Taylor's whistle, giving five minutes to compose ourselves and get behind our desks.

It was all a thirsty business and the drinking water facilities of that day were on a rota system. One of the senior boys would fill two buckets of water from the school pump, one placed in the outside wash house for the boys and one for the girl's cloakroom so, in a rush, we would all queue up, using the same chipped enamelled mug to quench our thirst.

There had been no celebration of the school sports in 1945, as it was cancelled because of the death of The Rev. Caddick-Adams, which caused a cloud of sadness throughout the Parish. So, the occasion of the school Sports Day of 1946 was also combined with a Victory Celebration which was held at Fauls on a field kindly loaned by Mr. Leslie Whitfield and with tea taken in the Church Hall afterwards. The arrangements for this special tea meant that food was provided by the parents, and the Woman's Voluntary Service (WVS) was also involved with the baking, making sure all tables were well laden. After which, the Vicar's wife, Mrs. Dentith, presented the prizes.

Fauls Green Church Hall

It had been a beautiful day with keen and enthusiastic competition, ensuring the large crowd of parents and well-wishers of the school were well entertained and with well laden tables of food, even if food was still supposed to be rationed, all enhanced by that wonderful feeling, at last we were at peace again!

Yes, peace and the return of loved ones, practically every family had a member who had served in some way, whether on active service or the local defence services.

George Mellor had been the first member of Fauls Parish to be called up and was involved in the early stages of the conflict in North Africa as a member of an artillery gun crew and unfortunately was taken prisoner. This was when Rommel and his Panzer Divisions were in the ascendancy, and George was to serve the fate of thousands of others, a concentration camp, and put to work in factories, as George was an engineer, or on farms. Now George was home, and as his friends commented that, during his war-time George had never had the opportunity to "spoil the shape of a good meal" and it was only the brilliant supply of Red Cross parcels that helped keep body and soul together.

George was to become a devout member of The Royal British Legion and on one occasion carried the Prees Branch banner at The Royal Albert Hall Festival of Remembrance. George was a gentleman by any standards, and later in life he suffered a stroke, after which he would drag himself around the adjacent 10-acre field twice a day, to retain as much mobility as was possible. George had been a pupil of Lower Heath School and a member of the prize-winning athletic team of the 1920's which had won The Royal British Legion Shield on five occasions, which is still a proud possession at the school.

** **Editor's Note**: Alvar Lidell was born to Swedish parents in Surrey in 1908 and was renowned as a BBC wartime newsreader and was the first Senior announcer for the BBC Third Programme, which became BBC Radio 3 in 1967.

CHAPTER 70

April, 2021: Road Safety and School Meals

On the 6th January 1946, Police Constable Arnold from Prees came to Lower Heath School and gave the children a talk on Road Safety, and expressed himself well pleased with the responses he received from the scholars. I was there, but left a month later, on my birthday. He then proceeded to examine the 23 bicycles and found that 17 of them needed attention. He came again in March to check them; hence the examination of bicycles was to become a regular occurrence by the school, with volunteer senior citizens helping to do the job.

At this time, Mrs. Patrick from the LEA, started to visit the school watching the various classes doing physical training and giving instruction on swimming. On the 25th June, 20 of the senior children were conveyed to Prees Heath swimming baths for the first time, with great excitement, and Mrs. Fearnall was in charge of these excursions.

Also, for the first time, children of eight years and under were conveyed to school by car from the outlying districts of Mickley and Northwood, with a comment from Mr. Bert Taylor that: "He did not think the driver was a very good judge of age!"

On the 25th November 1946, at 2.15 p.m. the Education Secretary called and inspected the building and enquired about the numbers on the register.

On the 3rd January 1947, there was a meeting of School Managers in the Church Hall at Fauls, when Mr. Abbotts from the Education Department attended to explain the development plan for this area, under the Education Act. This meeting was then opened to parents and supporters of the school, to hear what had been simmering since the 1930's. Lower Heath School was to be closed and he explained plans for the future. Here followed a big protest.

It appears Mr. Abbotts was entertained to a Geography lesson, explaining the strategic position of the school and the huge catchment area; exactly the same reasons why Dame Mary Hill left money for the building of Industry Hall in the late 18th century and which, of course, is still true today in 2021. Hence the only alterations to the status of the school were due to the increase in the school leaving age, when children at 14 were transferred to Broughall School, Whitchurch and eventually becoming a junior school with children leaving at 11. But this was not to happen until Mr. Bert Taylor's retirement in 1950.

With the future of the school now established, the need for the improvement of facilities was highlighted by the collapse of the school pump; the only means of a water supply. Mr. Bert Taylor wrote: "So, as it was urgent, I had a small rotary pump put in, which had to be constantly primed, also the well needs attention with surface water draining into it, parents are becoming very critical of the water supply here, it is also depressing for scholars and teachers." After discussions by the School Managers, it was decided to pipe the water from the well in the school house yard to the girl's cloakroom and the boy's wash bowl, thereby abolishing the carriage of drinking water in buckets, which had often been unfavourably commented on by the Medical Officer; estimates to be obtained.

"THERE IS ALWAYS A BOOK ON THE SHELF...!"

Also, the interior of the school had not been decorated for fifteen years – due to War time – and Mr. Bert Taylor was a bit put out by the School Architect, who appeared at the end of the day, walked through the school, round the outside with a quick glance at the roof and was for off. Then, Mr. Bert Taylor mentioned the need for interior decoration and his reply was, "Oh! We don't bother with that unless requested by the school managers."

The problems of the school provided a focal point for the school managers who instructed the correspondent to write to the Education Office, urging them to have the water supply analysed and provide canteen facilities for the scholars. At the same time requesting them to "make arrangements" for the decoration of the interior of the school and Messrs. Minshall (from Prees), Jones (from Whitchurch) and Minshall (from Market Drayton) were invited to tender, on the authority of the School Architect, who visited on the 22nd April 1947.

Although a school canteen had been mentioned previously, with architects having visited four times, eventually a blueprint was submitted, to which the school managers responded:

(a) no financial help could be given by the school managers
(b) no water supply was shown on the plans,
(c) a drain was shown being taken onto Mr. F. Davis's property,
(d) more would probably have to be done to the room than the architect had planned.

However, all is well that ends well and by November 1947, work was now progressing to put in place all those requirements from (a) to (d) and supplies for a canteen at Lower Heath School.

The children enjoyed their first meal on September 9th 1948. With the first school meals delivered from Wem, because the drainage was still not completed, all plates and cutlery had to be taken to Wem to be washed, except the knives. But from 14th February 1949, meals were brought from the Whitchurch Central Kitchens and Miss Kaye, the Canteen Inspector, became a regular visitor.

CHAPTER 71

May, 2021: Sandford Records Retained

At a meeting of the school managers on the 14th March 1947, Mrs. Athene Sandford informed them, that owing to her departure from the district, she had to resign from the committee and her position as Treasurer. She expressed her regrets that her association with the school had ended. The Chairman, in thanking Mrs. Sandford for her many years of service, referred to the Sandford family and their association with the school, practically from its inception, and that appreciation should be recorded.

Mrs. Athene Sandford had been the wife of the last Squire of Sandford, Leslie Gordon, whose family had been at Sandford for over eight centuries. She had also been a Sunday School teacher and involved herself in the local community, and having an excellent singing voice, formed the Prees Choir with the Rev. Caddick-Adams, and she was also a founder member of the Women's Institute and its first President.

On leaving Sandford in 1932 she lived at Marchamley with her three daughters – Armein, Alice and Elspeth. Armein on her retirement, and now a widow with the married name of Morrison, returned to live at Marchamley, where I had the privilege of getting to know her. Armein came to Sandford at the age of three, her father becoming what was to be the last Squire of Sandford, and leaving at the age of 19, so it was riveting to hear her reminisce about the days of the Sandford Estate, as a member of the family living in the Queen Anne Mansion.

Mrs. Athene Sandford and her three daughters pictured in front of their house at Marchamley

Those days, with Sandford still being the most picturesque of little villages, with its old water mill and charm of Tudor cottages, with the rooks hovering, still mostly horse drawn vehicles, and with motorised traffic only just starting to appear. Recorded on the admission register of Lower Heath School are a considerable number of children of the Sandford estate workers and tenantry, reminding me of what Mrs. Hockenhull told me: "The Sandford children came across the fields in a drove with Mrs. Evans the Infants teacher, who was also a tenant on the Estate, hand-in-hand with the younger ones, on their way to school."

Mrs. Morrison loved visiting her memories of Sandford, especially her early education when Mr. Bert Taylor would appear every Saturday morning at 9.00 a.m. prompt, to give

"THERE IS ALWAYS A BOOK ON THE SHELF...!"

lessons which she loved and never forgot, and eventually she went on to a private school. Mrs. Morrison, a wonderful bit of old Aristocracy, with no 'airs and graces,' no nonsense, had always worked for her living, and during the 1939/1945 War was involved working for the Navy, Army, and Air Force Institutes (NAAFI) at airfields in East Anglia, experiencing all the sadness of the non-return of familiar faces after bombing raids over Germany.

Her husband had been a doctor, who had also been the pilot of flying boats involved in mine laying in the North Sea. They had one daughter who lived at Baschurch, who she used to motor over to and visit until her eyesight started to fail. That journey was to take her past the Railway Inn at Yorton, where on occasions she loved to call, have a cup of tea, and reminisce with the two landladies, who had been the daughters of the Sandford Estate Gamekeeper.

However, at this time there was a family problem. Armein's sister Alice, who lived in New Zealand, had developed severe hip problems and, being unable to finance an operation, wanted to sell the Sandford family papers, which in 1939 had been deposited in the Shropshire Archives by their mother for safe keeping. An American University had offered £40,000 for them, unseen. Armein was very much against this, wanting them to stay in England as a permanent record for future scholars and historians. So, she rallied the family, including the Sandford's of the 'Isle of Bicton,' the paintings were sold and Alice was provided with a new hip and the over eight centuries of the Sandford family history stayed where they belonged, now permanently in the Shropshire County Archives in Shrewsbury.

There is a stone placed in the west elevation of Lower Heath School, now sadly illegible, informing us:

"This school was founded in 1799 by the Hill family of Hawkstone and maintained entirely by them until 1875." After those days, the Sandford family had become very influential in the welfare of the school.

Sadly, both the Hill and Sandford families lost their Estates through bankruptcy, the Hills in 1905 after three and a half centuries and the Sandford's in 1932 after eight centuries.

CHAPTER 72

June, 2021: Nibs and Inkwells

Once again, as I meander through Mr. Bert Taylor's many Log Book entries and especially his notebook, with his itemised agenda for his reports to the School Management Committee, it amazes me what volume of detail a Headteacher must take on board. However, now within sight of his retirement, he was to witness more change and progress to benefit education than he could ever have imagined during the austerity of the 1939/45 War. Thankfully, now well negotiated with the challenges of coping with the flood of Evacuees; at one spell there were over 200 youngsters, making it very difficult for teachers to teach and pupils to learn.

Of those times Enid Cumberlidge wrote, in her response to the Liverpool Echo advert: "I do wish I had not been an Evacuee as I missed the love and affection of my family, although that did not affect my life as such", this was because of the love and kindness she received from the Hill family of Ford Farm, Darliston – "but I feel from an educational point of view, I was deprived of two years education which took a number of years for me to regain".

Thankfully with all that in the past, the school having survived closure by the school authorities, the fortunes of Lower Heath scholars were set to unfold in a very pleasant way.

In 1947 when the school leaving age was raised to 15, it was pastures new for the last educational year scholars being transferred to Wem Modern School or Whitchurch Secondary

School. Also, with the Technical College and Radbrook Domestic Science College in Shrewsbury coming on stream, this gave more children the opportunity to sit exams at 13, so that they might attend there, and adding to the odd one or two that gained access to the Grammar or High School. For parents requiring boarding school facilities for their children, the Education Department at Shirehall accommodated Mellichope Hall at Corvedale as a secondary school for 35 boys.

Now, all this potential for further education, created an atmosphere of positivity so nicely reflected in Mr. Bert Taylor's reports to the School Managers: "After twelve months, attendance was at a record 89% and the children appeared to be much healthier." All scholars really enjoyed two days holiday to celebrate Princess Elizabeth's Wedding (20th November 1947), as indeed so did the whole country. He also wrote that the swimming lessons were very successful, children quickly acquiring the skill, becoming very competitive and achieving good grades with regular visits from the physical training instructors taking the classes; this all added to the fitness of the children.

Mr. Burt Taylor termed the introduction of a school canteen as a highlight. And, very importantly, the headmaster's reports mention the excellent work of Mrs. Ridgway and Mrs. S. Mellor – canteen helpers – in serving the meals. Part of the old Industry Hall was used as a dining room for the older children (40) whilst the infants partook of their meal in their classroom, which was not altogether ideal, but magic compared with hitherto. Miss Kaye now became a regular visitor inspecting the canteen facilities.

There was a bone of contention that had dragged on, that being the problem of the school repairs and maintenance, or lack of them, involving debates about aided schools and controlled schools. Lower Heath School, which had been the hub of activity for entertainment, the hiring charges for the premises providing income to help counteract the above problems. However, with the opening of Fauls Church Hall, that income was all but finished and the Education Authorities were seemingly very reluctant to take on board the full costs.

Obviously during the War years nothing was done, so by now the school had seen no decoration, as Mr. Bert Taylor wrote: "I hope some effort can be made to decorate the interior, 13 years since done, parents are equally critical of its state, I can assure you it is very depressing for the scholars and teachers to carry on in this condition". But it was not to be until the 12th January 1949, that Mr. Bert Taylor was able to make the log book entry: "Re-opened school – delayed from the 8th as the interior decorators had not finished".

Likewise, estimates were obtained for the exterior decoration, then returned for revision, but authority was not given to proceed until Spring of 1951, at a cost of £33 17s. 6d (worth £1057.19 in 2024, the equivalent of 23 days skilled tradesmen).

May 18th 1949 was to be the last inspection of the school by HMIS whilst Mr. Bert Taylor was the headmaster, with there being 82 children on the books. They mentioned that improvements noted in the last report had been fully maintained and in general the teaching ensures a satisfactory rate of progress. HMIS noted that the children's speech training is good and children enjoy recitation and there are some colourful expressions of art. Good responses were given to questions on History, Geography and Nature Study, and they liked the general tone and appearance of the children. They noted the interest shown in Literature: "there is now a need for further opportunities for freedom in the written exercises but more care is required with errors in spelling."

Oh! And they did not like the nibs the children were using.... it being still in the days of inkwells in every desk, which were filled by one of the senior boys every Monday morning. Biros being still for the future. They thought the rhythmic training is restricted when the weather is unfit to go into the playground, there being no gymnasium facilities. However, they noted with approval the gardening cultivation by the boys, but expressed a thought that the girls should be involved in garden instruction as well.

I too remember my first gardening lesson with Miss Parry, who would plant crocus bulbs in a pot and place them in the dark under the stairs, where the ink was also kept, and the excitement of monitoring their growth instilled in me the joys of planting seeds for ever. The most regular school visitor was Miss Heron, inspecting the garden plots, and for the first time I noticed she continued to bring 28lb. sacks of artificial manure!

CHAPTER 73

July/August, 2021: Retirement Announced

Extracts show that on the 8th April 1948, the school enjoyed a day's holiday to celebrate the King George VI and Queen Elizabeth's Silver Wedding Anniversary.

The entry for 15th October 1948, stated: "Seven scholars have been helping with the potato picking". This entry was to be the last recording of the age-old tradition, whereby children, pupils or scholars absented themselves from school, to be involved in potato planting, harvesting and the picking of damsons.

On the 8th July 1949, the school received another holiday, with lots of those children attending the Royal Show, held at Shrewsbury that year, attracted by the visitation of Princess Elizabeth and Prince Phillip, the Duke of Edinburgh.

Shrewsbury – Royal Visit, 1949 (Photo: Wellington Chronicle)

On the 9th September 1949, there was a meeting of School Managers at 3.45 p.m. in the school, The Rev. Harri Davies presiding. The headmaster gave his report, dealing with the various points of interest during the past year. Just over twelve months experience of school meals, which included further appreciation of the excellent work of Mrs. Ridgway and Mrs. S. Mellor. The success of several scholars in the Secondary School's examinations, a commendation by the Physical Training organiser for the district of the Physical Training undertaken and a report by HMIS following an inspection visit, were all touched on.

Mr. Bert Taylor also informed the Management Committee that he would be terminating his duties as Headmaster at the end of the Winter Term, i.e. at Easter 1950. He had commenced in the school as a pupil teacher 46 years ago that week and had completed 30 years as Headmaster the previous day. He hoped, at a future meeting, to thank them for their kind consideration and support during the past 30 years.

Mr. Bert Taylor wrote in his notes: "He would be giving the Chairman the necessary three months' notice early, to give them more time to notify the Education Office and for the Committee and the Authority to appoint my successor. I also thought the question of the tenancy of the schoolhouse might arise and it would give a longer period to solve that. I feel I ought to retire while I am doing useful work and I also feel that children today should have someone as Head, much younger than I can claim to be."

At the meeting of School Managers on the 5th December 1949, also present Mr. Quine from the Education Department; there had been only one application for the vacant headship next Easter. This was enlarged on by Mr. Quine, who suggested that after Easter 1950, senior scholars at eleven years plus should be transferred to Whitchurch Secondary Modern School. It was probable that more applications would be attracted and the older scholars would have the chance of participating in the practical instruction available in that type of school. This proposal was accepted by the school mangers unanimously, who also asked Mr. Bert Taylor if he would continue until the summer holiday, which he consented to do.

By March 9th 1950, the School Managers had received eight applications for Headteacher and, on 13th April, four of the applicants were invited for interview and it was decided to offer the position of Headmistress to Miss Blain, her duties to commence on 1st September next, whereupon the school would become a Junior School.

At those two meetings of the School Managers, it firmly established there was still a need and a future for the school at Lower Heath. This again emphasised the foresight of Dame Mary Hill. She had made funds available for the building of Industry Hall, which became Lower Heath School, on the waste lands of North Shropshire, to stop the youngsters running wild, to teach them to read, write, receive religious instruction and become useful in the workplace.

CHAPTER 74

September, 2021: "There is always a book on the shelf to help!"

With the delay in appointing Mr. Bert Taylor's successor, he had willingly agreed to continue for another term. This was to be a term of adjustment in the status of Lower Heath School in the process of becoming a Junior School. Mr. Hargreaves, Head of Whitchurch Secondary Modern School at Broughall, and Mr. Pugh – school Attendance Officer – called to see readers text books and other items now not required at Lower Heath school and said they would be pleased to accept all and take them to Broughall, where, of course, all Mr. Bert Taylors pupils over 11 years old now were.

I am sure those pupils would have taken memories away of their last sports day with Mr. Bert Taylor, who always brought a lot of emphasis and encouragement to the subject, which had taken place on the 21st July 1949. The sports had been held on Mr. Cyril Darlington's field, the children bringing the ingredients for tea, which was prepared under the supervision of Mrs. Taylor and the ex-WVS members. Mrs. Harri Davies of Fauls' Vicarage presented the prizes. The senior scholars then presented the headmaster with a pocket lighter.

So, Mr. Bert Taylor's last extra term also involved the first Sports Day as a Junior School, which was held on 18th July 1950, which was a repeat of the above, but Mrs. Byrd presented the prizes. Also, as Mrs. Fearnall was retiring, she was presented with a handbag and tea service by the scholars and teachers.

"THERE IS ALWAYS A BOOK ON THE SHELF...!"

On the 28th July 1950 Mr. Bert Taylor's log book entry said: "School closed for summer holidays, Mr. R.B. Taylor (Bert) retired from teaching and terminated his duties as Headmaster."

20th August 1950: (Copy of letter received from Mr. Martin Wilson, Secretary for Education).

"I have been looking at the record of your service in Shropshire and have observed that you first began duty at Little Drayton School as long ago as May, 1915 (previously he had held posts in Welshpool and Wellington). This has been a long period of service in the cause of education in the County and I feel that the occasion must not pass without letting you know how much your work has been appreciated. I have no doubt that the children of Lower Heath will have cause to be grateful to you for what has been done on their behalf. Your help has been greatly valued and the readiness with which you agreed to continue as Headmaster when your successor had not been appointed, was very much appreciated. On behalf of the Committee and staff of the Office, I send you best wishes and would express the hope that you will have many years of happy retirement.

Yours sincerely,
H. Martin Wilson."

With Mr. Bert Taylor's retirement, the link between Lower Heath School, with father and son holding the position of headmaster for an unbroken 75 years, came to an end. In fact, Mr. Bert Taylor had completed 46 years in the profession, which commenced when he was appointed as a pupil teacher at the school and later studied at Saltley College, Birmingham, and succeeding his father as headmaster in 1919.

Mr. Bert Taylor, like his father, had taken a great part in the public, church, and social life of the district. He had been secretary of Prees Cottagers Cow Club since 1929, and was secretary and treasurer of the Hospitals Contributory Scheme in Fauls Parish until the new National Health Service came into effect in 1948. He was a member of Prees Parish Council and had taken a prominent part in organising social events and entertainment in the district. So, it was a very pleasing ceremony which took place in Fauls Church Hall to mark Mr. Bert Taylor's retirement, with many of his old scholars and a wide circle of friends who had congregated to convey their best wishes.

The Rev. Harri Davies presided and the presentations, which consisted of three cheques amounting to £64 4s. 6d., were made by Mrs. Black on behalf of the Managers, Joan Ward, and Joyce Mapp on behalf of scholars and staff, and the Chairman on behalf of the former pupils, parishioners, and well-wishers. The Hall was packed for the occasion and many tributes recognising the recipient's service to the school and district were paid. Janet Dutton presented a bouquet to Mrs. Taylor and both suitably replied for the gifts and kind wishes. Afterwards, Mr. & Mrs. Taylor entertained the company, which numbered some 300, for refreshments. Sadly, I was unable to be one of that number, being with British Army of the Rhine (BAOR) in Germany, doing National Service.

However, I have been forever appreciative of his influence on my life with his encouragement to achieve to the best of one's ability, and his advice: *"There is always a book on the shelf to help if you want to learn more Roger!"*

"THERE IS ALWAYS A BOOK ON THE SHELF...!"

Headmaster Mr. Bert Taylor Presenting at Sports Day

And so now ends the first 150 years of the school's progress, with three Roberts accounting for 113 of those years as Headmasters. Robert Goffin – 39 years; Robert Taylor senior – 44 years; Robert Taylor junior – 30 years.

As I write these 70 years on, I am sure they would have all been very pleased that Lower Heath School is still in full flow, with a dedicated Headteacher and staff, and with over one hundred children in attendance.

It being a wonderful testament to the Hill family of Hawkstone, the idea of financing the school by Dame Mary Hill, and the building of it by her stepson Sir Richard Hill. Also instrumental in the progress of the school, the Rev. Brian Hill, Elizabeth Hill, and Viscountess Anne Hill, who doubled the size of the school and ensured it was fully maintained by the family for the first 75 years.

www.ingramcontent.com/pod-product-compliance
Lightning Source LLC
Chambersburg PA
CBHW032101090426
42743CB00007B/201